Adaptive Intelligence for Cloud Content Delivery

By

Davidoff

CONTENT

CHAPTER 1

Introduction

This chapter presents the concepts of peer-to-peer video content downloading, highlighting the need for enhancing video content delivery, the challenges faced in P2P systems, and the potential of cloud-based solutions. It outlines the research motivation, objectives, and organization of the thesis, setting the stage for a comprehensive exploration of advanced video downloading methodologies.

1.1 Introduction

Media, in its various forms, plays a crucial role in modern society by informing, educating, and entertaining audiences (**Li et al., 2021**). It shapes public opinion, influences culture, and serves as a platform for communication and expression. Media's pervasive presence impacts virtually every aspect of daily life, from social interactions to political discourse. Within this landscape, video content downloading has become an integral part of digital media consumption, allowing users to access and enjoy video content offline. This is particularly important in areas with limited or unreliable internet connectivity. It enhances the flexibility of media consumption, enabling users to watch content on the go without the need for continuous internet access.

The latest trends in video content downloading reflect significant advancements and evolving user needs. With improvements in video compression technology, users can now download high-definition (HD) and 4K content more efficiently, maintaining high quality while minimizing file size. Major spilling platforms alike Netflix, Amazon Prime Video, and Disney+ have exploited on this by offering offline viewing options, allowing subscribers to download content for later consumption (**Falkowski et al., 2020**). Enhanced peer-to-peer protocols facilitate faster and more reliable downloads by leveraging distributed networks, reducing the load on central servers. Additionally, cloud-based solutions deliver scalable and secure storage options for downloaded content, making it accessible across multiple devices. The combination of Artificial Intelligence (AI) and machine learning further optimizes video compression, enhances download speeds, and personalizes content recommendations for offline viewing.

The future of video content downloading is promising, driven by several key factors. As mobile devices become more powerful and ubiquitous, the demand for downloadable video content is expected to grow, particularly in emerging markets. The rollout of 5G networks will significantly enhance download speeds and reduce latency, making high-quality video downloads more accessible and efficient. Continued advancements in video compression algorithms will enable even higher quality downloads at lower data costs, making it feasible to store extensive video libraries offline. As the Internet of Things (IoT) ecosystem expands, video content downloading will become more integrated with smart home devices, enabling seamless content consumption across different platforms (**Nguyen et al., 2020**). With growing awareness of environmental impacts, there will be a push towards more energy-efficient downloading methods, potentially driving innovation in this space. Additionally, evolving data privacy and copyright regulations will shape the future landscape of video content downloading, balancing user accessibility with content protection. Overall, the significance of video content downloading continues to grow, driven by technological advancements and changing consumer behaviors. Its future scope promises further innovations, enhanced user experiences, and broader accessibility, solidifying its place as a vital component of digital media consumption.

1.1.1 Evolution of Media Consumption

The trajectory of media consumption has undergone significant transformations over the past few decades. Initially, media consumption was largely passive and linear, with audiences constrained by scheduled broadcasts and limited content availability. The advent of the internet introduced interactive and on-demand media consumption, empowering users to access a wide array of content tailored to their preferences and schedules.

With the emergence of Web 2.0, user-generated content became a cornerstone of media consumption, fostering participatory cultures and democratizing content creation. Social media platforms facilitated real-time sharing and interaction, further blurring the lines between content creators and consumers. This participatory model has led to diverse content landscapes, catering to niche interests and fostering global communities

1.1.2 The rise of Video Content

Video content, in particular, has experienced exponential growth due to its engaging and immersive nature. Advances in video production technologies, coupled with decreasing costs of equipment and software, have lowered barriers to entry for content creators. Additionally, improvements in internet infrastructure, such as the deployment of fiber-optic networks and the advent of 5G technology, have enhanced the capacity for streaming high-definition and ultra-high-definition video content seamlessly.

According to recent statistics, video content is projected to account for over 80% of all internet traffic, highlighting its dominance in the digital media landscape. This trend is further accentuated by the growing popularity of live streaming, virtual reality (VR), and augmented reality (AR) content, which offer immersive experiences across various domains, including entertainment, education, and professional training.

1.1.3 Importance of Video Content Downloading

While streaming remains a prevalent mode of video content consumption, downloading video content has maintained its relevance and importance. Video content downloading enables users to access and enjoy media offline, providing flexibility and convenience, especially in contexts where internet connectivity is limited, unreliable, or expensive. This capability is crucial for users in remote or underdeveloped regions and for those who wish to consume content during travel or in settings without stable internet access.

Moreover, downloading video content allows for better control over data usage, enabling users to download content during off-peak hours or when connected to Wi-Fi, thereby managing bandwidth consumption effectively. It also facilitates uninterrupted viewing experiences, free from buffering issues and quality degradation that may occur during streaming due to fluctuating network conditions.

1.1.4 Advancements in Video Content Downloading Technologies

Recent advancements in video content downloading technologies have significantly enhanced the efficiency and quality of downloaded media. Innovations in video compression algorithms, such as H.265 (HEVC) and AV1, have enabled high-definition and 4K content to be compressed into smaller file sizes without substantial loss in quality, making downloads faster and more storage-efficient (**Falkowski et al., 2020**).

Leading streaming platforms have integrated sophisticated downloading features into their services, offering users the ability to download and store content for offline viewing seamlessly. These platforms employ adaptive bitrate streaming and smart downloading strategies that optimize download speeds and manage storage effectively. Additionally, the integration of Artificial Intelligence and Machine Learning technologies has facilitated personalized content recommendations and predictive pre-fetching, enhancing user engagement and satisfaction.

1.1.5 Impact of emerging technologies on video content downloading

Emerging technologies are poised to further revolutionize video content downloading. The deployment of 5G networks promises significantly higher download speeds and lower latency, enabling the rapid transfer of large video files and supporting real-time downloading of high-resolution and immersive content. Edge computing and cloud-based services are enhancing content delivery efficiency by processing and storing data closer to the end-users, reducing latency and network congestion.

Furthermore, blockchain technology offers innovative solutions for secure and decentralized content distribution, addressing concerns related to data security, privacy, and content ownership. Smart contracts and decentralized storage systems can facilitate transparent and tamper-proof transactions, ensuring fair compensation for content creators and secure access for consumers.

1.1.6 Challenges and Opportunities in video content downloading

Despite these advancements, video content downloading faces several challenges, including issues related to copyright infringement, security vulnerabilities, and resource management. Ensuring equitable access to high-quality content while safeguarding intellectual property rights and maintaining network efficiency remains a complex endeavor. However, these challenges also present opportunities for innovation and the development of robust, secure, and efficient content delivery systems that cater to diverse user needs and contexts.

1.1.7 Future Prospects of video content downloading

Looking ahead, the future of video content downloading is anticipated to be shaped by continued technological innovation and evolving consumer behaviors. Integration with Internet of Things ecosystems will enable seamless content consumption across a multitude of connected devices, enhancing user convenience and engagement. Advancements in AI and ML will further personalize and optimize content delivery, improving user experiences and operational efficiency.

Environmental sustainability is also emerging as a critical consideration, with efforts directed towards developing energy-efficient downloading and storage solutions to minimize the carbon footprint associated with digital media consumption. Collaborative initiatives among technology developers, content providers, and policymakers will be essential in navigating the complexities and harnessing the full potential of video content downloading in the digital age.

1.2 Peer-to-Peer Video Content Downloading

The concept of P2P networks emerged in the late 1990s and early 2000s with platforms like Napster, which revolutionized file sharing by enabling users to share music files directly. Subsequent P2P applications, such as BitTorrent, expanded this model to include various types of digital content, including video files, and introduced more sophisticated protocols to enhance efficiency and reliability. Peer-to-peer video content downloading has become a significant part of digital distribution, allowing users to part and transfer video files directly from one another without the need for centralized servers. This decentralized approach has gained widespread popularity due to several factors, including the expansion of internet connectivity globally and the varied range of content available on P2P networks, such as user-generated videos **(Jin et al., 2021).**

Despite legal concerns that surrounds copyright issues, the appeal of P2P video content downloading remains strong between users seeking convenient and accessible ways to access a variety of content. P2P networks operate on the principle that each participant contributes resources, such as bandwidth and storage, facilitating a collaborative ecosystem where all users benefit from shared contributions. This contrasts with traditional client-server models, where a central server is responsible for distributing content to multiple clients, often leading to bottlenecks and scalability issues during high-demand periods.

A typical architecture of P2P video downloading is given in **Fig. 1.1** P2P video downloading architecture comprises several key components:

- **Peers:** Individual users connected to the network who share and download video files.
- **Trackers:** Servers that facilitate communication between peers by maintaining lists of available peers and coordinating file sharing activities.
- **Swarm:** A group of peers sharing the same file, collectively contributing to the distribution and downloading process.
- **Pieces/Chunks:** Video files are divided into smaller segments or chunks, enabling simultaneous downloading from multiple peers and facilitating efficient data transfer.

Some of the advantages of P2P video content downloading are as follows:

(i) ***Efficiency and Scalability***: P2P networks distribute the load among multiple peers rather than depending on a dominant server. This decentralization can significantly enhance efficiency and scalability, especially for popular content, as the more users there are, the more resources are available for distribution.

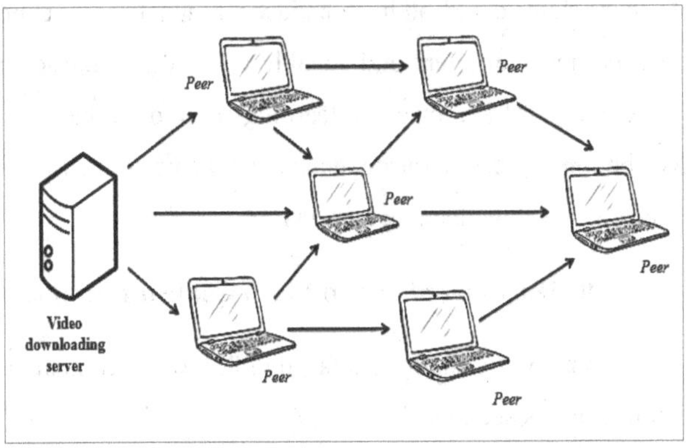

Fig. 1.1 Peer-to-peer video downloading

(ii) ***Cost Reduction***: By leveraging the computing and bandwidth resources of individual users, P2P reduces the reliance on costly centralized infrastructure, leading to potential cost savings for service providers and users.

(iii) ***Redundancy and Reliability***: P2P networks inherently provide redundancy. If one peer goes offline, the content can still be downloaded from other peers, enhancing the overall reliability and availability of the content.

(iv) ***Bandwidth Optimization***: P2P networks can optimize bandwidth usage by dynamically distributing data from multiple sources, potentially improving download speeds for users with varying internet connection qualities.

The future of P2P video content downloading looks promising with the advent of new technologies and methodologies. Advances in blockchain technology could offer solutions to some of the security and incentive issues by providing decentralized and transparent ledger systems for tracking contributions and ensuring fair compensation (**Liu et al., 2008**). Integration with 5G technology could address bandwidth and latency concerns, making P2P networks more efficient and capable of handling high-quality video streams. Additionally, AI and machine learning could optimize peer selection and data distribution processes, further enhancing the performance and reliability of P2P video content downloading systems.

1.3 Challenges faced in P2p Video Content Downloading

Some of the challenges faced in P2P video content downloading are outlined in this section.

1.3.1 Network Topology and Performance Variability

P2P networks often consist of peers with varying network conditions. Variations in peer availability and network performance can cause irregular download speeds and disruptions. High latency in communication between peers can negatively impact the efficiency and speed of video content downloading, particularly for time-sensitive streaming (**AlTuhafi et al., 2013**).

1.3.2 Resource Management

Managing bandwidth allocation among multiple peers can be complex, especially when peers have different upload and download capacities. Poor bandwidth management can lead to suboptimal performance. Peers need sufficient storage space to cache and share video content. Limited storage on user devices can restrict the amount of content that can be shared and downloaded.

1.3.3 Peer Behavior and Participation

In P2P networks, some users may consume resources without contributing back, a behavior known as free-riding. This can reduce the overall efficiency and availability of content in the network. The frequent joining and leaving of peers (churn) can disrupt the stability and reliability of the network, making it challenging to maintain consistent download streams (**Hisada et al., 2010**).

1.3.4 Content Integrity and Quality Control

In P2P networks, video content is often broken into small fragments for distribution. Ensuring that all fragments are correctly assembled and maintaining the integrity of the video can be challenging. The video content quality can differ based on the source peers (**Lou et al., 2012**). Ensuring consistent quality across downloads requires effective quality control mechanisms.

1.3.5 Legal and Ethical Issues

P2P networks must navigate complex legal landscapes that vary by region. Ensuring compliance with copyright laws and other regulations can be difficult, particularly when content is distributed globally.P2P networks can be used to distribute inappropriate or illegal content. Implementing effective content moderation to prevent the spread of such material is a significant challenge.

1.3.6 Technical Complexities

Different P2P applications may use different protocols, leading to compatibility issues. Ensuring interoperability between various P2P systems can be technically challenging (**Liu et al., 2007**). Managing different versions of the same video content in a distributed network can be complex. Ensuring that users download the latest or correct version requires sophisticated version control mechanisms.

1.3.7 Economic and Incentive Models

Designing and maintaining effective incentive models that encourage users to contribute resources to the network is critical (**Manzato et al., 2014**). Without adequate incentives, user participation may decline. Developing viable monetization strategies for content creators and distributors within a P2P framework can be challenging, especially given the decentralized nature of the network.

1.3.8 User Experience and Interface

P2P applications need to be user-friendly to ensure widespread adoption. Complex interfaces and difficult setup processes can deter users from participating in P2P networks (**Wu et al., 2005**). Providing adequate technical support for users encountering issues with P2P video content downloading can be challenging, especially in decentralized networks without a central authority.

1.4 Need for Enhancing Video Content Downloading

The need for enhancing video content downloading stems from several factors related to technological advancements, user expectations, and the evolving digital landscape. Here are a few key reasons why there is a pressing need to improve video content downloading:

1.4.1 Demand for high-quality content

As consumers demand higher resolution content, the file sizes for video downloads increase. Enhancing video downloading capabilities ensures that users can efficiently download HD and UHD content without excessive waiting times or consuming excessive bandwidth. The rise of VR and AR content, which requires even more bandwidth and storage, underscores the need for more efficient downloading mechanisms (**Wu et al., 2013**).

1.4.2 Accessibility and connectivity

In many parts of the world, consistent high-speed internet access is not available. Enhancing video downloading can provide users with the ability to download content when they have access to a stable connection and watch it offline, ensuring a flatter and more inclusive viewing experience. With the proliferation of mobile devices, there is a growing need for downloading capabilities that cater to the constraints of mobile data plans and the need for offline viewing.

1.4.3 User convenience and experience

Users increasingly consume media on the go, during commutes, or in locations without internet access. Enhancing video downloading ensures they can access their favorite content anytime, anywhere, without interruption. In the age of instant gratification, users expect quick and seamless access to content. Improved downloading speeds and efficiency contribute to a better user experience (**Ullah et al., 2011**).

1.4.4 Cost Efficiency

Enhanced video downloading can optimize the use of available bandwidth, reducing the load on networks and lowering costs for both service providers and consumers. By improving the efficiency of content distribution, there is less need for expensive infrastructure investments, such as additional servers and data centers.

1.4.5 Environmental Considerations

More efficient downloading methods can lower the energy consumption involved in data transfer and storage, thereby promoting environmental sustainability (**Chism et al., 2009**). By optimizing the downloading process, the overall carbon footprint of digital content distribution can be minimized.

1.4.6 Technological Advancements

The rollout of 5G networks and advancements in edge computing offer opportunities to enhance video downloading by reducing latency and increasing download speeds, making it possible to handle larger files and more users simultaneously. Continued development in video compression algorithms can reduce file sizes without compromising quality, enabling faster downloads and less storage usage.

1.4.7 Content Distribution and Scalability

Enhancing video downloading supports the efficient distribution of content on a global scale, ensuring that users in different regions can access content quickly and reliably (**Lima et al., 2012**). Improved P2P downloading mechanisms can enhance scalability and reduce the reliance on centralized servers, distributing the load across a network of users.

1.4.8 Data Security and Privacy

Enhancements in video downloading can incorporate better safety measures to guard user information and guarantee protected dealings (**Sanchez et al., 2010**). Improved downloading technologies can help meet stringent data privacy regulations, ensuring that content providers and users remain compliant with laws such as GDPR.

1.5 Strategies to Improve Video Content Downloading

Improving video content downloading can be approached from various angles beyond caching, bandwidth management, and caching mechanisms. Following are several strategies to improve video content downloading:

1.5.1 Adaptive Bitrate Streaming (ABR)

Adaptive Bitrate Streaming is a methodology utilized in video streaming that enhances the watching occurrence by vigorously modifying the video feature in real-time according to the user's present set-up surroundings (**Wei et al., 2024**). ABR streaming architecture is given in **Fig. 1.2**. Following are key components of ABR:

(A) Dynamic Streaming: Dynamic streaming is a key component of ABR. It automatically adjusts the video quality to match the user's internet speed and stability. If a user's internet connection is fast and stable, the video will be streamed at a higher quality, ensuring a clear and sharp picture. If the connection slows down or becomes unstable, the video quality is reduced to prevent buffering and interruptions. This ensures continuous playback, minimizing the chances of the video stopping or stuttering.

(B) Multi-bitrate Encoding: Multi-bitrate encoding is another essential aspect of ABR. Videos is encoded at multiple bitrates and resolutions during the preparation stage. This means that several versions of the same video are created, each at a different quality level. The video player can then switch between these different streams in real-time, based on the available bandwidth. For example, if a user's bandwidth drops, the player will automatically switch to a lower bitrate stream to maintain smooth playback. Contrariwise, if more bandwidth becomes available, the player will switch to a higher bitrate stream, improving video quality.

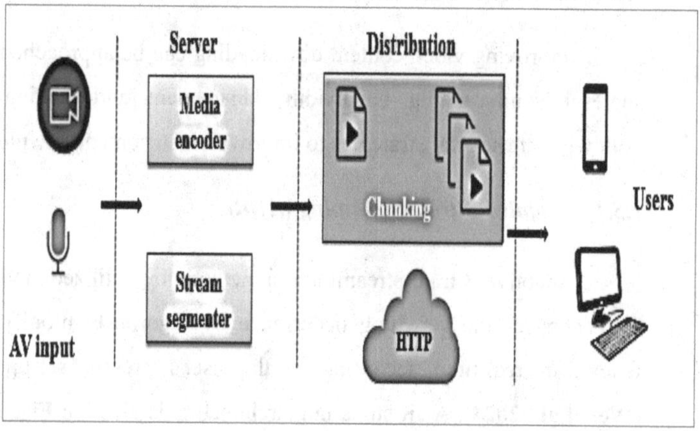

Fig. 1.2 ABR Streaming framework

1.5.2 Content Delivery Networks (CDNs)

Content Delivery Networks are systems of distributed servers that deliver web content to users based on their geographic location. CDNs are essential for enhancing the performance, speed, and reliability of websites and online services. A simple CDN example is given in **Fig. 1.3**.

(A) ***Edge Servers:*** Edge servers are strategically located servers that are part of a CDN. These servers are placed nearer to end users to decrease the distance that data must transportable. When user requests content, the CDN directs the request to the nearest edge server, minimizing latency and significantly improving download speeds. This proximity decreases the time it takes for the data to reach the user, leading to faster loading times and a more responsive experience (**Pruthvi et al., 2024**).

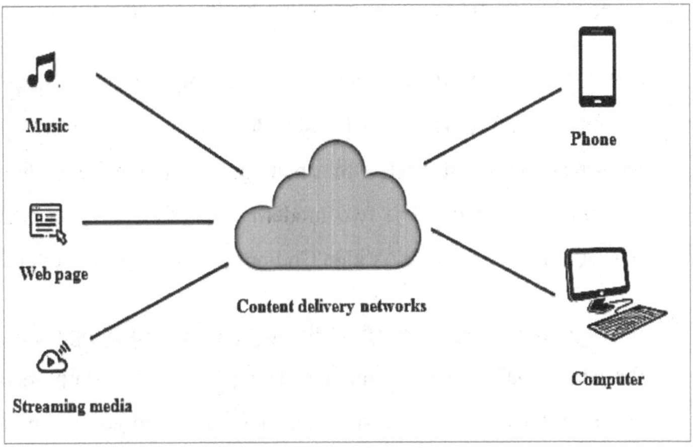

Fig. 1.3 CDN example

(B) ***Load Balancing:*** It is a technique used by CDN to distribute incoming network traffic across multiple servers. This distribution ensures that no single server becomes overwhelmed with too many requests. By spreading the load, CDN can handle high traffic volumes more effectively, prevent server overloads, and maintain high performance and availability. Load balancing also helps to enhance fault tolerance and reliability, as traffic can be redirected to other servers in case one server fails or becomes overloaded. This balanced approach ensures a smooth and uninterrupted user experience, even during peak traffic times or unexpected surges in demand.

1.5.3 Data Compression

Data compression is a crucial technique in video streaming and downloading, aimed at reducing the file size of videos without sacrificing quality. This makes it possible to stream and download videos more efficiently, especially over networks with varying bandwidth capacities.

(A) Efficient Codecs: Video codecs are algorithms used to compress and decompress digital video. Efficient codecs decrease the quantity of information required to represent a video, thus making the files smaller without significantly affecting the quality. The two modern and efficient video codecs are H.265 (HEVC - High Efficiency Video Coding) and VP9 (**Grois et al., 2016**).

(B) Transcoding: It refers to the method of renovating video files from one format or quality level to another. This is essential for optimizing videos for different devices and network conditions. The main goals of transcoding are to balance quality and file size, ensuring faster downloads and smoother streaming.

1.5.4 Parallel Downloads

Parallel downloads involve dividing a video file into smaller segments that can be downloaded simultaneously. This approach enhances the overall download speed and efficiency.

(A) Chunking: Chunking is the process of breaking a video file into minor, more manageable pieces or "chunks." These chunks are downloaded simultaneously rather than sequentially, which speeds up the download process.

(B) HTTP/2: It is a major revision of the HTTP network protocol used by the World Wide Web. It introduces multiplexing, which allows multiple requests and responses to be sent over a single connection simultaneously. This capability greatly enhances the efficiency of parallel downloads. A HTTP chunked framework is depicted in **Fig. 1.4**.

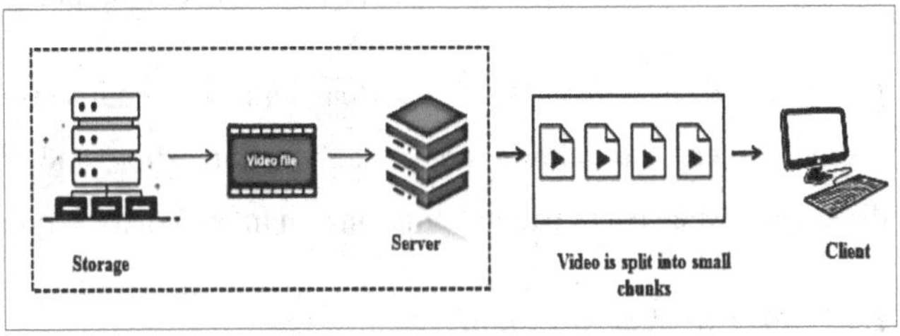

Fig. 1.4 HTTP Chunked Encoding Framework

1.5.5 Progressive Downloading

Progressive downloading allows users to begin watching a video before the entire file has been downloaded. This technique enhances the user experience by providing immediate access to video content.

(A) Partial Playback: Partial playback means that as soon as the initial chunks of a video are downloaded, the user can begin watching the video. The rest of the video continues to download in the background.

(B) Range Requests: HTTP range requests allow clients to demand specific portions (or ranges) of a video file from a server. This feature is critical for enabling partial playback and efficient downloading.

1.5.6 Optimized Delivery Protocols

Optimized delivery protocols are essential for improving the speed and efficiency of video streaming and downloading. These protocols leverage advanced networking techniques to reduce latency, increase throughput, and enhance the overall user experience.

(A) ***QUIC Protocol:*** QUIC (Quick UDP Internet Connections) is a transport layer network protocol designed by Google to provide faster and more efficient internet connections than traditional TCP (**Kharat et al., 2018**).

(B) ***WebRTC:*** WebRTC (Web Real-Time Communication) is an open-source project that allows real-time communication and video streaming directly between peers without requiring an intermediary server.

1.5.7 Peer-to-Peer Streaming

This technique leverages the assets of distinct customer devices to distribute video content more efficiently. This approach can enhance scalability and download speeds, particularly in high-demand scenarios.

(A) ***Hybrid CDN:*** Hybrid Content Delivery Networks combine traditional CDN infrastructure with P2P technology (**Jiang et al., 2016**). This hybrid approach offers several benefits such as load distribution, enhanced availability, and cost efficiency and so on.

(B) ***Mesh Networks:*** Mesh networks are decentralized networks where users share downloaded video segments with each other. This approach enhances the efficiency and speed of content delivery.

1.5.8 Edge Computing

Cao et al., (2020) proposed edge computing as a distributed computing paradigm that brings computation and data storage closer to the location where it is needed. This is particularly beneficial for video streaming and downloading, as it can significantly reduce latency and improve speed.

(A) ***Local Processing:*** Edge computing entails processing data nearer to the end user, at the network's edge. By processing video content at local servers or devices near the user, the time it takes for data to travel back and forth between the user and a central server is minimized. This results in reduced latency and improved speed.

(B) ***Edge Caching:*** Edge caching involves storing frequently accessed video content on servers located close to the users. This strategy ensures that popular videos are readily available; reducing the need for repeated long-distance data transfers. Benefits of edge caching include faster access and reduced server load.

1.5.9 Pre-fetching and Predictive Loading

Pre-fetching and predictive loading are techniques used to anticipate user needs and load content in advance, ensuring a seamless viewing experience.

(A) ***Predictive Algorithms:*** Predictive algorithms analyze user behavior and patterns to forecast what content a user is likely to watch next. By pre-fetching this content in the background, users experience seamless transitions and improved experience.

(B) ***User Behavior Analysis:*** Analyzing user behavior helps in understanding viewing habits and preferences. This information can be used to intelligently pre-load content that a user is likely to watch.

1.5.10 Efficient Network Protocols

Efficient network protocols are designed to optimize data transfer, ensuring that video content is delivered quickly and reliably.

(A) ***Optimized TCP:*** TCP (Transmission Control Protocol) is a fundamental protocol for internet data transfer. Optimized versions, such as Bottleneck

Bandwidth and Round-trip propagation time, improve throughput and reduce latency (**Claypool et al., 2018**).

(B) ***Network Coding:*** Network coding involves encoding data in a way that enhances error correction and data recovery during transmission. This technique offers improved reliability, efficient transmission and so on.

1.5.11 Video Optimization Techniques

Video optimization techniques are employed to adjust video settings dynamically, ensuring the best possible quality based on various factors.

(A) ***Dynamic Resolution:*** Adjusting the video resolution constructed on the device's screen size and network conditions ensures optimal viewing.

(B) ***Content-aware Encoding:*** Using machine learning to optimize encoding settings based on the content of the video.

1.5.12 User Interface Improvements

Improving the user interface can greatly enhance the user experience by providing useful information and options.

(A) ***Buffer Indicators:*** Clear indicators of buffering status and video quality help manage user expectations.

(B) ***Download Options:*** Offering users the option to download videos for offline viewing at different quality levels provides flexibility and convenience.

1.6 Cloud-Based Video Content Downloading

Cloud-based video content downloading (**Li et al., 2021**) has dramatically transformed the landscape of digital media distribution and consumption. By utilizing the extensive infrastructure of cloud computing, this approach facilitates the efficient storage, management, and delivery of video content on a global scale. Unlike traditional centralized servers or peer-to-peer networks, cloud-based systems capitalize on the robust capabilities of globally distributed data centers, ensuring video content is highly accessible, scalable, and consistently available. The transition to cloud-based downloading is propelled by the increasing demand for high-quality video content, including high-definition (HD), ultra high-definition (UHD), and cutting-edge formats like virtual reality and augmented reality.

One of the most significant advantages of cloud-based video content downloading is its dynamic scalability. Cloud infrastructure offers elastic resources, enabling service providers to manage large spikes in user activity without compromising performance (**Evangeline et al., 2015**). This scalability is crucial for streaming platforms that must accommodate millions of concurrent users. Moreover, cloud-based solutions often integrate with content delivery networks, which cache content closer to end-users. This integration reduces latency, enhances download speeds, and ensures a seamless viewing experience. The global reach of cloud services ensures that users, regardless of their geographic location, can access content quickly and reliably (**Shen et al., 2010**).

Despite its advantages, the shift to cloud-based video content downloading presents several challenges. Managing costs can be complex, particularly with the pay-as-you-go model, which may lead to unforeseen expenses during periods of high demand. Additionally, ensuring data privacy and complying with regional regulations add layers of complexity, as does maintaining robust security against cyber threats. However, the benefits of cloud-based video content downloading—such as improved performance, reliability, and scalability—make it a compelling option for content providers (**Hefeeda et al., 2015**). As technology continues to evolve, advancements in cloud computing, edge computing, and artificial intelligence are expected to further enhance these systems, solidifying cloud-based downloading as a central component of the digital media landscape. A cloud-based video content downloading scenario is given in **Fig. 1.5**.

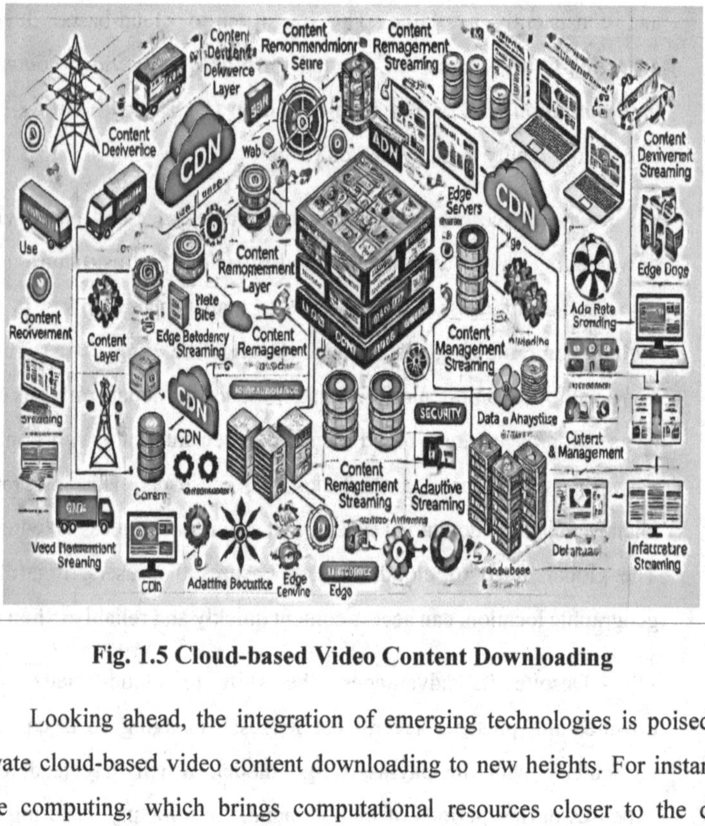

Fig. 1.5 Cloud-based Video Content Downloading

Looking ahead, the integration of emerging technologies is poised to elevate cloud-based video content downloading to new heights. For instance, edge computing, which brings computational resources closer to the data source, is expected to reduce latency even further and improve the efficiency of video content delivery. Additionally, artificial intelligence and machine learning are being increasingly employed to optimize content distribution, predict user demand, and personalize content recommendations, thereby enhancing the overall user experience. The convergence of these technologies with cloud-based downloading promises to address existing challenges while opening new possibilities for content providers and consumers alike. The detailed architecture of cloud-based video content downloading showcasing the layers is given in **Fig. 1.6**.

(1) User-Interface Layer

- ***Web/Mobile App Interface:*** It is the platform through which users interact with the service, browsing and requesting video content.

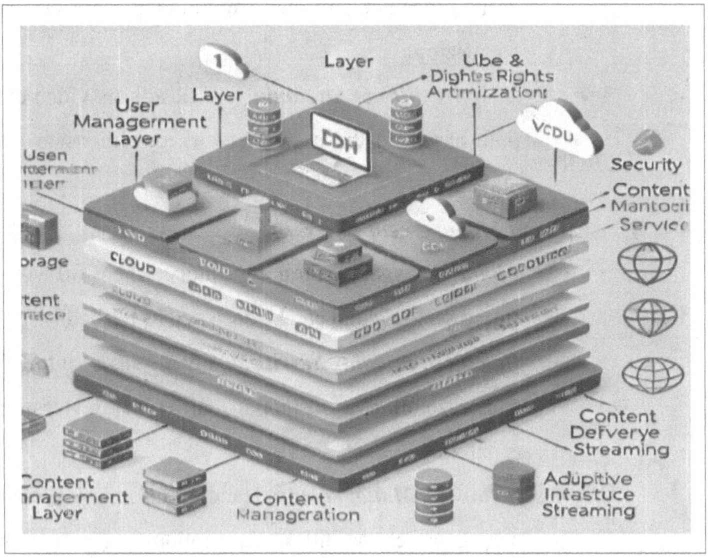

Fig. 1.6 Detailed Architecture of Cloud-Based Video Content Downloading

- ***Content Recommendation Engine*****:** It suggests personalized content to users based on their viewing history and preferences using data from the Data Processing Layer.

- ***User Authentication and Authorization:*** This module verifies user identities and manages access permissions to ensure secure and authorized content access.

(2) Content Delivery Layer

- ***Content Delivery Network*:** CDN distributes video content across geographically dispersed servers to reduce latency and improve download speeds.
- ***Edge Servers:*** These servers make cache content closer to the user's location, further minimizing latency and network congestion.
- ***Adaptive Bitrate Streaming*:** ABR adjusts video quality in real-time based on the user's network conditions to ensure smooth playback.

(3) Content Management Layer

- ***Cloud Storage*:** Central repository where all video content is stored securely and can be accessed as needed.
- ***Video Transcoding Service:*** Converts videos into various formats and resolutions to support different devices and network capabilities.
- ***Metadata Management:*** Handles information about the video content, such as titles, descriptions, tags, and indexing for efficient search and organization.
- ***Data Redundancy and Backup:*** Ensures data is replicated and backed up across multiple locations to prevent loss and ensure high availability.

(4) Data Processing Layer

- ***Machine Learning Algorithms*:** These ML algorithms are used to analyze user data to improve content recommendations, predict trends, and optimize delivery.

- ***Real-Time Analytics:*** Monitor system performance and user interactions to make informed decisions and adjustments dynamically.
- ***Content Analytics Engine*:** Provides insights into content performance, user engagement, and helps in strategic planning for content creation and distribution.

(5) Security Layer

- ***Encryption Services*:** Protects data during storage and transmission to prevent unauthorized access and data breaches.
- ***Access Control and DRM:*** Manages and enforces policies regarding who can access and use the video content, ensuring compliance with licensing agreements.
- ***Blockchain Integration:*** Adds an additional layer of security and transparency in transactions and content distribution, enabling immutable tracking and verification.

(6) Cloud Infrastructure Layer

- ***Elastic Compute Services:*** Provides scalable computing resources that can adjust according to the workload demands, ensuring efficient performance.
- ***Load Balancers:*** Distribute network traffic evenly across servers to prevent overloads and maintain optimal performance.
- ***Database Services:*** Store and manage structured data such as user profiles, transaction records, and system logs with high reliability.

(7) Monitoring and Management Layer

- ***Performance Monitoring:*** Continuously observes the health and performance of all system components, identifying and addressing issues proactively.

- ***Logging and Auditing:*** Keeps detailed records of system activities and user interactions for security audits, compliance, and troubleshooting.
- ***Auto-Scaling Services:*** Automatically adjusts resource allocation based on real-time demand, optimizing cost and performance.

1.6.1 Cloud Storage and Video Content Management

Primarily, cloud-based video content downloading offer hybrid Storage Solutions that explore how hybrid storage systems that combine on-premise and cloud-based solutions can optimize video content management, offering both flexibility and security. Additionally, data Redundancy and Backup feature discusses the importance of redundancy in cloud storage, which ensures that video content is always available, even in the case of hardware failure. Finally, cloud-based video content downloading stream offers lifecycle Management that examines the strategies for managing the lifecycle of video content in the cloud, including archiving, retrieval, and deletion processes.

1.6.2 Security in Cloud-Based Video Content Downloading

When it comes to security in cloud-based video content downloading, encryption and secure transmission strategies like detail encryption protocols are used to secure video content during download and streaming, preventing unauthorized access. Following which, access control mechanisms like role-based access controls (RBAC) is utilized to ensure that only authorized users can download or view specific video content.

1.6.3 AI and ML in Cloud-Based Video Downloading

As stated earlier, AI and ML are revolutionizing the domain of cloud video downloading, whereas the first concept comes the predictive analytics for user preferences that discusses how machine learning models can predict user preferences and optimize video content delivery by preloading content that a user is likely to watch. Secondarily, real-time analytics and content recommendations explores how real-time analytics are driven by AI and can be used to recommend video content based on viewing history and user behavior. Finally, automated Quality Enhancement is utilized in examining machine learning algorithms that automatically enhance video quality, adjust bitrates, or perform dynamic compression to improve the user experience.

1.6.4 Blockchain in Cloud-Based Video Content Downloading

In cloud-based video content downloading, blockchain technology is used in decentralized content distribution. It is also used in analyzing how blockchain technology can be used to create a decentralized network for video content distribution, ensuring transparency and reducing the risk of piracy. Apart from that, it finds application in smart contracts for licensing and payment that addresses the potential of smart contracts to automate licensing agreements and payments for video content, streamlining transactions and ensuring fair compensation for content creators. Finally, immutable content tracking can be carried out that explores how blockchain can be utilized to track the origin and distribution path of video content, ensuring that all copies are legitimate and that content integrity is maintained.

1.6.5 Cloud-Based Video Content Downloading and Edge Computing

Integrated with cloud video downloading, edge storage solutions is offered in this stream by examining how edge computing can complement cloud-based downloading by storing frequently accessed video content closer to the user, reducing latency. Collaborative edge-cloud architecture that integrates edge and cloud computing in video content downloading, allows cloud servers to handle large-scale processing, and edge devices in managing real-time, localized tasks. Also, to explore the role of edge devices in processing video content before delivery, such as transcoding or compressing video streams to optimize delivery speed and quality is another advantage of edge computing in the domain of video content downloading.

1.7 Problem Statement and Research Motivation

Scalability of existing methods to house the increasing volume of customers and content diversity remains a critical constraint. Current video content downloading systems often struggle with efficient resource utilization, resulting in prolonged downloading times and degraded user experiences. Traditional caching mechanisms in peer-to-peer systems may not adequately address the dynamic needs of content distribution, often lacking robust predictive capabilities to anticipate user behavior and pre-cache content effectively. This leads to suboptimal resource allocation and performance inefficiencies.

The drive behind this research is the growing significance of video content downloading within the digital media landscape. While video streaming services have surged in popularity, downloading continues to be a preferred option for many users due to its offline accessibility and convenience for sharing. Despite its advantages, existing video content downloading systems face significant challenges, such as scalability issues, extended downloading times, and inefficient resource utilization. By addressing these issues and enhancing system performance, this research aims to bridge the gap between user expectations and current system capabilities.

This research seeks to contribute innovative solutions that improve the efficiency, scalability, and overall user experience of video content downloading. By focusing on advanced predictive mechanisms and dynamic resource allocation strategies, the study aims to meet the evolving needs of modern media consumers. The ultimate goal is to develop robust, scalable systems that can efficiently handle the increasing demand and content diversity, thereby aligning with the ever-changing landscape of digital media consumption.

1.8 Research Objectives

The research aims to achieve the three following objectives:

(1) To investigate and implement techniques utilizing Eye OS and Content Distribution Techniques to enhance the video content downloading time in cloud-based systems, particularly focusing on improving throughput as the number of peer entities increases.

(2) To develop pioneering caching strategies to a mass often viewed content faster to users, thereby improving overall system performance in cloud-based video content downloading and minimizing the download time in turn.

(3) To explore the integration of machine learning techniques to develop predictive caching mechanisms that anticipate user requests and content popularity, preemptively caching content closer to potential requesters to enhance system efficiency and reduce download times.

1.9 Overall Architectural Diagram of the Research

The **fig 1.7** describes the overall architectural diagram of the research. As shown below the raw data is given as input where Data collection: The system collects the necessary data that will be used in the decision-making process.

Feature extraction: From the collected data, relevant features are extracted. These features are critical attributes or variables that will be used to train the decision tree model. This phase includes

Training data preparation: The extracted features are then prepared into a suitable format for training the decision tree model. This might include splitting the data into training and testing sets, normalizing, or encoding categorical variables.

Model training: Using the prepared training data, the decision tree model is trained. The model learns patterns and relationships from the data to make future predictions or decisions

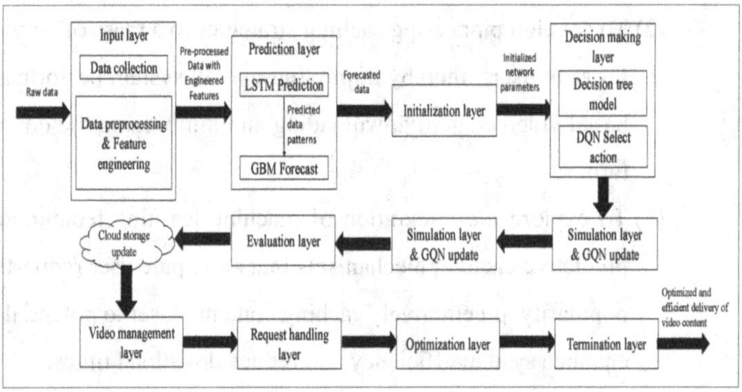

Fig. 1.7 Detailed Architecture of the Research Work

Model evaluation: After training, the model is evaluated to determine its accuracy and effectiveness. This might involve using a separate test set to check how well the model performs on unseen data and calculating metrics such as accuracy, precision, recall, and F1 score.

Data distribution decision making: Based on the trained and evaluated model, the system makes decisions regarding data distribution. This step involves using the model to predict or decide how data should be distributed across various nodes or servers.

Continuous learning and adoption: The system continuously learns and adapts. This means that it periodically collects new data, updates its feature extraction process, retrains the model, and adjusts its data distribution decisions based on new insights and feedback.

In the next phase the Dynamic Adaptive Caching and Distribution Engine model architecture is a sophisticated system designed to optimize caching and distribution decisions using a combination of machine learning and reinforcement learning techniques

Pre-process data feature engineering: The initial step involves preparing the data through feature engineering. This includes cleaning the data, extracting relevant features, and transforming the data into a format suitable for the model. Feature engineering is crucial as it directly impacts the model's performance.

LSTM predict GBM forecast:

(1) LSTM predict: A Long Short-Term Memory (LSTM) network is used to predict future data patterns. LSTM is effective for time-series forecasting due to its ability to remember long-term dependencies.

(2) GBM forecast: A Gradient Boosting Machine (GBM) is then used to make forecasts based on the LSTM predictions. GBM is a powerful ensemble machine learning technique that builds models sequentially to improve accuracy.

- ***Initialize network state:*** The network's initial state is set up. This involves defining the parameters and environment in which the model will operate, essentially setting the stage for the decision-making process.

- ***DQN select action:*** A Deep Q-Network (DQN) is used to select the best action. DQN is a reinforcement learning algorithm that combines Q-Learning with deep neural networks to learn optimal policies for decision-making in complex environments.
- ***Simulate action:*** The selected action is simulated in the environment. This step involves applying the action to see its effect on the system, allowing the model to gather feedback on the action's impact.
- ***Update GQN:*** The model is updated based on the action's outcome. This likely involves a Generative Q-Network (GQN) or a similar mechanism that incorporates the feedback from the simulation to refine its decision-making process.
- ***Check termination condition:*** The system checks whether the termination condition has been met. This could be based on specific criteria such as achieving a certain performance level or running for a predefined number of iterations.
- ***Continue/Optimize decisions*:** If the termination condition is not met, the process loops back to optimize decisions further. The system continues to refine its actions and update its models iteratively.

The process concludes once the termination condition is satisfied, indicating that the model has reached an optimal state or the desired performance criteria.

This architecture leverages advanced machine learning techniques like LSTM, GBM, and DQN, combined with continuous simulation and updating, to create an adaptive and optimized caching and distribution engine. The system is designed to learn and adapt dynamically, ensuring efficient and effective data distribution decisions.

1.10 Overall Flow Diagram of the Research

The flow diagram as shown in the **Fig 1.8** outlines the various steps involved in a research or computational process, combining data analysis, machine learning models, reinforcement learning, and decision-making procedures. Here's an overview of each step and its role in the overall workflow:

(i) Start: The process initiates.

(ii) Data Collection: Collect relevant data for the system

(iii) Pre-process Data Feature Engineering: Prepare and engineer features from the collected data for better model performance.

(iv) LSTM Predict GBM Forecast

(a) LSTM Predict: Use LSTM to predict future data patterns.

(b) GBM Forecast: Use GBM to forecast based on LSTM predictions.

(v) Initialize Network State: Set up the initial parameters and environment.

(vi) Decision Tree Model Training and Evaluation: Train and evaluate the decision tree model for making data distribution decisions.

(vii) DQN Select Action: Use DQN to select the best action based on the current state.

(viii) Simulate Action: Simulate the chosen action to understand its impact.

(ix) Update GQN: Update the model based on the results of the simulated action

(x) Is the Active Video Less Than k?:

(i) Yes: Proceed to update the cloud storage.

(ii) No: Return to the start and re-evaluate.

(xi) Update Cloud Storage to Add Video by Replacing Video Without Request: Add a new video to the cloud storage, replacing one that has no current requests

(xii) N1 = N1 + Nj: Update the metric N1N1N1 by adding NjNjNj

(xiii) Is (H / (N1 + ajNj)) < NjU?:

(a) Yes: Use helper mode for video jjj.

(b) No: Block peers requesting video jjj as server mode and return to the start

(xiv) Use Helper Mode for Video j: Implement helper mode for video jjj.

(xv) Is Cu[i] == 'IDLE'?:

(a) Yes: Serve the request for video jjj.

(b) No: Hold the request until Cu[i]Cu[i]Cu[i] is 'IDLE'.

(xvi) Serve the Request Video j: Provide the requested video.

(xvii) Request will be Held Until Cu[i] == 'IDLE': Hold the request and update N1N1N1

(xviii) N1 = N1 + ajNj: Further update N1N1N1.

(xix) Continue/Optimize Decisions: Loop back to optimize decisions based on feedback.

(xx) Check Termination Condition: Check if the termination criteria are met.

(xxi) End: Conclude the process if the termination criteria are satisfied

This process emphasizes a loop of continuous feedback and decision-making, with a focus on machine learning techniques like LSTM, GBM, and reinforcement learning (DQN) to optimize actions and predictions

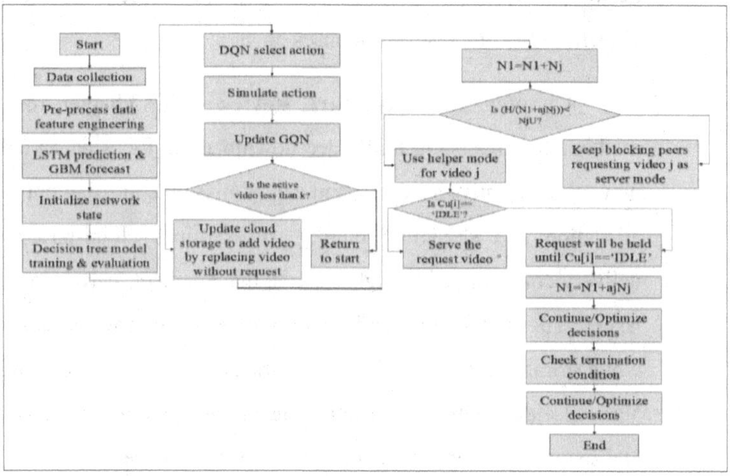

Fig. 1.8 Overall Flow Diagram of the Research

This combined architecture leverages the strengths of LSTM and GBM for forecasting, Decision Tree models for initial decision-making, and DQN for adaptive action selection and optimization, creating a robust and dynamic system for efficient data caching and distribution.

1.11 Organization of the Thesis

Chapter 1 – Introduction: This chapter introduces the foundational concepts of video content downloading with a meticulous importance on P2P systems and the emerging significance of cloud-based solutions. It begins by discussing the vital role of media in modern society and the rising importance of video content downloading as a means to improve accessibility and user convenience. The chapter then explores current trends, challenges, and future prospects of video content downloading, highlighting the advancements in compression technology, the integration of AI, and the implications of 5G networks. The motivation behind the research is presented along with the key objectives that the research focuses on.

Chapter 2 – Literature Review: This chapter reviews advanced methods for enhancing P2P video downloading, focusing on balanced overlay networks, incentive schemes, and call admission control to optimize bandwidth allocation and streaming quality. It examines cloud-based video content delivery constraints, highlighting cost management, performance, and security issues. The architecture and benefits of Eye OS are discussed, emphasizing cloud storage, content delivery networks, and adaptive streaming technologies. Various video content distribution techniques, including CDN, P2P methods, and secure streaming protocols, are explored for their efficiency in optimizing performance. The chapter also covers innovative caching mechanisms and the application of machine learning, such as reinforcement learning and LSTM networks, to improve caching strategies and user experience. Further, it explores advanced techniques and algorithms aimed at optimizing video streaming and downloading processes across diverse network environments and devices. The review further delves into video content downloading algorithms highlighting their capabilities in adaptive streaming and load balancing. Methods to optimize P2P video downloading, such as balanced overlay networks and incentive schemes, are explored alongside considerations for cloud-based video content delivery, addressing cost management, security, and scalability.

Chapter 3 – Adaptive Cloud Downloads: This chapter explores the Enhanced Automated Mode Selection algorithm, integrated within the Eye OS cloud environment to optimize video downloads. It details EAMS dynamic mode selection, toggling between server and assistant modes based on real-time conditions, significantly improving download speeds. Empirical evaluations show EAMS achieving rapid download times across various network speeds. The adaptive behavior of EAMS, selecting server or P2P modes as needed, ensures a 100% success rate in video downloads. The chapter highlights EAMS efficiency, scalability, and effectiveness in enhancing real-time video content delivery through advanced caching and adaptive algorithms.

Chapter 4 – Optimized Cloud Download Service: This chapter introduces an intelligent caching mechanism that reduces download latency by strategically caching popular video content closer to end-users, dynamically updating based on real-time popularity metrics. It explores a data distribution algorithm using decision tree models for optimizing video delivery across P2P networks, adapting strategies based on network conditions and user behaviors to maximize download speeds. Additionally, it presents a bandwidth resource organization technique that automatically reserves bandwidth based on video quality requirements and user preferences, ensuring equitable resource allocation and enhancing the streaming experience. Experimental evaluations demonstrate the effectiveness of these techniques in reducing download times, improving cache hit ratios, and enhancing overall system performance across varied network conditions.

Chapter 5 – Integrating Machine Learning In Peer-to-Peer Video Content Systems for Predictive Caching and Dynamic Data Distribution: This chapter introduces the Dynamic Adaptive Caching and Distribution Engine, a machine learning-driven approach to enhance P2P video content delivery. D-ACADE comprises three modules: Content Popularity Prediction for proactive caching using LSTM networks, User Demand Forecasting with gradient boosting machines, and Resource Optimization using deep Q-networks for real-time data distribution. By predicting content popularity and user demand, and dynamically optimizing network resources, D-ACADE reduces download times, buffering delays, and network load. The chapter emphasizes D-ACADE adaptability, scalability, efficiency, and cost-effectiveness in improving user experience in P2P video streaming.

Chapter 6 – Conclusion and Scope for Further Study: This chapter discusses the conclusion and future scope of the research work, focusing on enhancing cloud services and video streaming technologies. It highlights the improvements in productivity, storage solutions, and data resilience offered by cloud services, along with the importance of robust security measures. For video streaming, it emphasizes the advancements in adaptive systems, machine learning integration, and robust encryption mechanisms. The chapter outlines future research directions to further enhance user experience, security, and system performance across evolving network landscapes.

CHAPTER 2

Literature Survey

2.1 Introduction

This chapter reviews advanced methods for enhancing peer-to-peer video downloading, constraints in cloud-based video content delivery, the architecture and benefits of Eye OS, various video content distribution techniques, innovative caching mechanisms, and the application of machine learning in improving caching strategies.

2.2 Methods for Improvising Peer-To-Peer Video Downloading

In a P2P video downloading process, ensuring sufficient bandwidth to all peers is essential. **Venkatraman et al., (2006)** proposed forming a balanced overlay network which aims to achieve full bandwidth utilization by ensuring that each peer's transmission load is proportional to its upload capability and is maintained within a local region. However, this method does not account for the bandwidth capacities of other peers, limiting its effectiveness in achieving global load balance. **Sung et al., (2006)** proposed an incentive scheme for P2P video streaming, forming an overlay multicast tree with branches of equal capacity. This system incentivizes peers to upload by maintaining incoming branches proportional to outgoing ones, encouraging download rates proportional to upload rates.

Kumar et al., (2007) and **Huang et al., (2007)** addressed this challenge through the deployment of call admission control (CAC). **Kumar et al., (2007)** utilized A fluid-flow model is used to analyze video streaming quality in P2P systems with two types of peers, assuming full utilization of peer upload bandwidth to determine the maximum attainable playback rate. They proposed adopting admission control when overall bandwidth is insufficient, ensuring that bandwidth demand does not surpass supply. **Huang et al., (2007)** classified P2P VoD networks into surplus, balanced, or deficit modes based on the relationship between bandwidth supply and demand. They contended that ideal system performance is achieved in the balanced mode, where supply and demand are equal.,

Small et al., (2007) suggested using a greedy algorithm called Outreach to paradigm the overlay mesh topology. Outreach connects new peers to deputy peers and selects parent nodes with the largest available bandwidth. However, its myopic operations may result in sub-optimal parental peer selection, making global optimum performance problematic to achieve. Beyond ensuring sufficient overall bandwidth, it is essential to allot bandwidth and implement quality of service at the peer level. **Wu et al., (2005)** explored this through mathematical programming approaches that jointly optimize topology construction and resource allocation. This method selects optimal construction combinations between peers and assigns data transmission rates. However, the iterative adaptations and intensive peer communications required make it costly for large-scale, dynamic P2P networks. This concern led to research by **Magharei et al., (2009)** on incremental topology formation, which refines the overlay topology locally to adapt to peer churn without altering other peers. The author also demonstrated that constructing an optimal mesh topology for video streaming, where each peer maintains an acceptable range of outgoing connections proportional to its upload bandwidth, ensures optimal bandwidth utilization and minimal buffer requirements. Simulations showed that the network performs best when per-connection bandwidth is uniform, avoiding bottleneck connections.

Lastly, **Kwong et al., (2008)** introduced a basic random walk outline is employed for P2P topology formation, offering mathematical analysis for heterogeneous P2P networks. This framework aims to improve the overall structure and efficiency of P2P video downloading by addressing the diverse capabilities of network peers.

Table 2.1 summarizes the key focus, strengths, and limitations of each approach for optimizing P2P video downloading processes. Each method offers unique strategies to enhance bandwidth utilization, ensure quality of service, and optimize network efficiency based on different computational models and network conditions.

Table 2.1 Comparison of Various Approaches for Optimizing P2P Video Downloading Processes

Approach	Focus	Strengths	Limitations
Balanced Overlay Network	Full bandwidth utilization	Proportional transmission load	Does not consider bandwidth capacities of other peers, limiting global load balance effectiveness
Incentive Scheme with Overlay Multicast Tree	Equalizing upload and download rates	Incentivizes proportional download rates to upload rates	Requires effective incentive mechanisms to maintain balance
Call Admission Control	Bandwidth management	Ensures video streaming quality through bandwidth control	Requires accurate fluid-flow models for optimal performance
Greedy Algorithm Outreach	Overlay mesh topology construction	Connects peers based on available bandwidth, forming efficient topology	Myopic operations may lead to sub-optimal parental peer selection
Mathematical Programming for Resource Allocation	Topology and resource optimization	Jointly optimizes topology and resource allocation	Intensive peer communications and iterative adaptations can be costly
Incremental Topology Formation	Adaptive overlay topology	Refines topology locally to adapt to peer churn, minimal buffer requirements	Focuses on local refinements, may not optimize global network performance
Random Walk Framework	Efficiency in heterogeneous networks	Improves overall structure and efficiency through mathematical analysis	Effectiveness depends on network heterogeneity and random walk parameters

2.3 Constraints of Cloud-Based Video Content Downloading

The growing demand for video content downloading has been significantly supported by cloud computing technology. Cloud providers offer a variety of services which allows video content providers to outsource their computational needs, thus avoiding the substantial costs and operational challenges of maintaining in-house infrastructure (**Li et al., 2017**). As a result, many video content download services have become heavily reliant on cloud solutions for their computing requirements (**He et al., 2013**). However, this dependence on cloud services introduces new challenges, particularly in managing costs, as these services typically operate on a pay-as-you-go model (**Lopes et al., 2022**). Video content providers must find a balance between minimizing expenses and sustaining a high Quality of Experience (QoE) for users. Research has delved into optimizing cloud expenditures and enhancing efficiency, focusing on aspects such as video transcoding costs (**Liet al., 2016**), video segmentation models (**Jokhio et al., 2011**), and resource provisioning methods like virtual machine allocation (**Lin et al., 2013**). While these studies offer valuable insights, a comprehensive approach is needed to streamline the entire video content downloading workflow using cloud services.

Cloud-based video content downloading, while offering significant benefits in terms of scalability and efficiency, faces several constraints that impact its implementation and performance. A primary concern is cost management, as cloud services operate on a pay-as-you-go pricing model, which can lead to unpredictable expenses, particularly with the high data transfer costs associated with large video files. Performance issues such as latency and bandwidth limitations also pose significant challenges, affecting download speeds and user experience. Ensuring scalability to handle peak demand periods is crucial for maintaining performance. Additionally, security and privacy are critical, with the need for robust data protection measures and compliance with regulations like GDPR (**Liu et al., 2003**). Technical challenges include the seamless integration of cloud services with existing systems, maintaining high reliability, and managing substantial storage and computational resources required for video processing tasks like transcoding and encoding (**Zhuang et al., 2012**). Furthermore, dependency on a single cloud provider can lead to vendor lock-in, complicating the ability to switch providers or ensure interoperability between different platforms. Effective content delivery, requiring extensive content delivery networks and caching strategies, is essential for minimizing latency and ensuring fast download speeds for a global audience. Addressing these constraints through careful planning and optimization is vital for leveraging the full potential of cloud-based video content downloading.

In essence, while cloud computing offers substantial benefits for video content downloading by providing scalable and efficient services, it also necessitates careful cost management and continuous optimization to ensure a seamless user experience. Further research is required to integrate various findings into a holistic strategy that optimizes cloud usage across all facets of video content downloading.

2.4 Eye OS in Video Content Downloading

EyeOS provides a unified platform where video content can be stored, managed, and delivered. The integration of cloud computing with video content downloading offers several benefits, including scalability, reduced latency, and improved user experience. In this framework, the core components include cloud storage, content delivery networks, edge computing, and adaptive streaming technologies.

2.4.1 Architecture of Eye OS

The architecture of Eye OS for video content downloading is designed to leverage the advantages of cloud computing, edge computing, and adaptive streaming technologies. The system is structured into several layers, each serving a specific function to ensure efficient and seamless delivery, storage, and streaming of video content. The architecture of Eye OS is illustrated in **Fig. 2.1.**

(A) ***User-interface layer*:** At the top, the user interface layer provides a web-based desktop environment accessible through web browsers. This interface is user-friendly, allowing users to manage their video content, initiate downloads, and stream videos directly. It also integrates media players for seamless video playback, ***Application layer*:** eliminating the need for external applications.

(B) Beneath the interface, the application layer comprises various tools and services essential for video content management. This includes video management tools for uploading, organizing, and editing videos. A download manager is also present to handle video downloads, offering functionalities such as pausing, resuming, and scheduling. Additionally, streaming services support both live and on-demand streaming, utilizing adaptive bitrate technology to ensure optimal playback quality based on real-time network conditions and device competences.

(C) ***Service layer*:** This layer is crucial for the efficient distribution and processing of video content. It includes a Content Delivery Network that distributes video content across multiple edge servers. By caching popular content close to users, CDN significantly reduce latency and enhance download speeds. Edge computing nodes in this layer further process and deliver video content from servers nearer to end-users, decreasing the load on central servers and minimizing latency. Adaptive bitrate streaming technology in this layer energetically adjusts video quality to match the user's available bandwidth and device competences, ensuring flat playback.

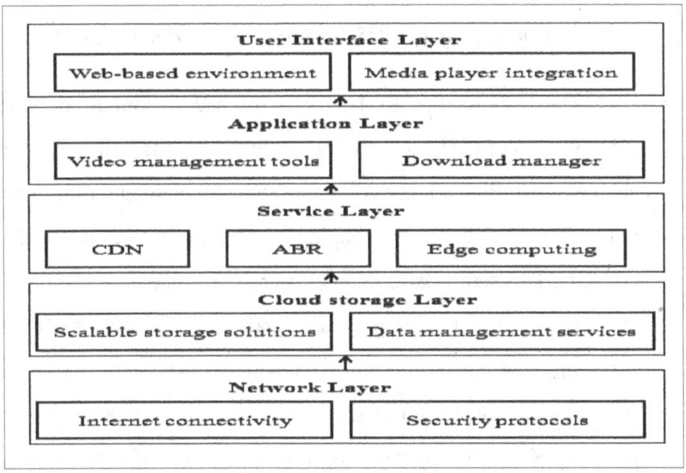

Fig. 2.1 Architecture of Eye OS

***(D) Cloud storage layer*:** The cloud storage layer provides scalable storage solutions, capable of handling vast amounts of video content. It ensures high availability and redundancy, protecting against data loss. Data management services within this layer handle metadata, indexing, and retrieval of video content, facilitating quick access and efficient storage utilization.

***(E) Network layer*:** At the base, the network layer provides the necessary infrastructure for high-speed video downloading and streaming. This includes robust internet connectivity to support the required bandwidth. Additionally, this layer implements security protocols such as HTTPS and RTMPS to ensure data integrity and confidentiality during transmission. These secure transmission protocols, combined with encryption mechanisms, protect video content from unauthorized access and distribution.

Each layer has its own specific functions, working together to ensure efficient content delivery, management, and playback while maintaining security and scalability.

2.4.2 Advantages of Eye OS in video content downloading

The architecture of Eye OS for video content downloading offers numerous benefits. Scalability is achieved through the cloud infrastructure, capable of handling a large volume of video content and user requests. Reduced latency is accomplished by bringing content closer to users via edge computing and CDN. This setup also enhances user experience through adaptive streaming, that ensures optimal video playback quality on the basis of network conditions. Furthermore, security is reinforced with secure protocols and encryption to protect video content. Accessibility is another key advantage, as users can operate their video content from any device with an internet connection, providing flexibility and convenience.

2.5 Video Content Distribution Techniques

Content Delivery Networks have proven to be critical in enhancing video downloading by leveraging edge caching to store copies of video content at nodes closer to end-users. This technique significantly reduces latency and improves download speeds (**Hu et al., 2016**). Additionally, the dynamic content distribution mechanism in CDN automatically distributes and replicates content across nodes based on demand and network conditions, further optimizing performance. Peer-to-Peer distribution techniques, such as those explored by **Tewari et al., (2007)** with the BitTorrent protocol, revolutionize video file distribution. By breaking down video files into smaller pieces that can be downloaded from multiple sources simultaneously, this approach increases download speeds and alleviates the load on central servers. Swarming techniques complement this by enabling users to share pieces of video files with each other, further accelerating the download process and enhancing network efficiency. A basic content distribution model utilizing CDN is given in the **Fig. 2.2**.

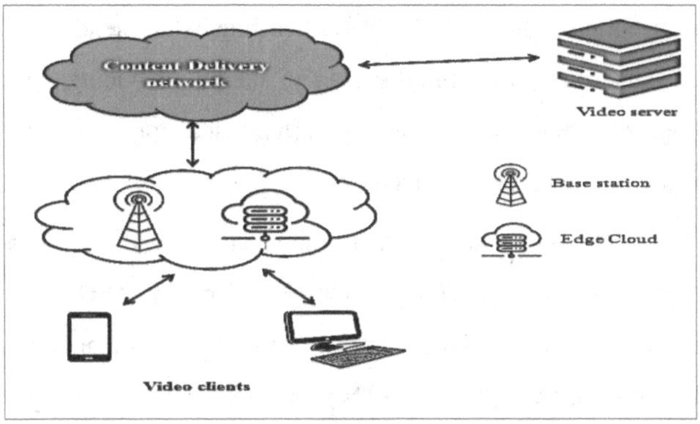

Fig. 2.2 Content Distribution Model using CDN

In addressing the need for real-time adaptability, **Sani et al., (2017)** highlight Adaptive Bitrate Streaming (ABR) as a key method. ABR enthusiastically adjusts video quality based on the user's accessible bandwidth and device capabilities, encoding videos at various resolutions and bitrates to ensure an optimal viewing experience across different network conditions. **Pathan et al., (2014)** emphasize the advantages of cloud-based distribution, which utilizes cloud storage and computing to store and process video content, ensuring scalability and reliability. Integrating edge computing, content can be processed and delivered nearer to end-users, thus dropping latency and improving download speeds.

Yetgi et al., (2012) present progressive downloading as a prominent distribution technique, allowing users to start watching videos while they download incrementally. This approach minimizes waiting times and, when combined with chunked file transfer, confirms a smooth viewing experience even under fluctuating network conditions. The hybrid content distribution model, as demonstrated by **Farahani et al., (2023)**, combines the reliability of CDN and the efficiency of P2P sharing. This method optimizes content delivery by utilizing both edge and cloud resources, tailored to user location and network conditions. Similarly, **Setton et al., (2007)** discuss multicast and broadcast distribution techniques like IP multicasting, which sends a solitary video stream to numerous users simultaneously, thereby reducing bandwidth usage for popular content. Broadcasting, often used for live events, reaches large audiences with minimal latency.

Securing video content from unauthorized access is **vital Liu et al., (2003)** explain that Digital Rights Management (DRM) systems encrypt and control access to video content, while secure streaming protocols such as HTTPS **(Geng et al., 2024)** and RTMPS ensure data integrity and confidentiality during transmission. Caching strategies play an essential role in optimizing storage usage and content availability. **Hasslinger et al., (2018)** describe the Least Recently Used (LRU) caching strategy, which keeps recently accessed content readily available while evicting older content. Popularity-based caching ensures frequently accessed videos are stored closer to end-users, thereby improving retrieval times

Quality of Service and Quality of Experience optimization are crucial for maintaining high standards of video delivery. **Devlic et al., (2015)** discuss how bandwidth management dynamically allocates network resources to ensure smooth playback and reduce buffering. Continuous QoE monitoring and adaptation help assess user experience and adjust content delivery strategies accordingly. Finally, **Shariff et al., (2017)** explore predictive and pre-fetching techniques that employ machine learning to anticipate user behavior and cache likely-to-be-requested content in advance. These pre-fetching strategies download video segments ahead of time based on user viewing patterns and network conditions, reducing delays and enhancing the overall viewing experience.

Table 2.2 shows the Comparison of different Video Distribution Techniques on various metrics such as Implementation cost, accuracy, flexibility and compatibility.

Table 2.2 Comparison of Video Distribution Techniques

Technique	Implementation Cost	Accuracy	Flexibility	Compatibility
Content Delivery Networks	High	High	Moderate	High
Peer-to-Peer Distribution (BitTorrent)	Low	Moderate	High	Moderate
Adaptive Bitrate Streaming	Moderate	High	High	High
Progressive Downloading	Low	Moderate	Low	High
Hybrid Content Distribution	High	High	High	High
Cloud-based Distribution	High	High	High	High
Multicast and Broadcast Distribution	Moderate	Moderate	Low	Moderate
Digital Rights Management	High	High	Low	High
Caching Strategies (LRU, Popularity-based)	Low to Moderate	High	Moderate	High
Quality of Service (QoS) and Quality of Experience (QoE) Optimization	Moderate	High	High	High
Predictive and Pre-fetching Techniques	Moderate	High	High	High

2.6 Caching Mechanisms in Video Content Downloading

Integrating cloud and caching functions at the network edge has revolutionized content delivery, offering users significantly reduced latency **(Xia et al., 2021). Han et al., (2021)** delved into the complexities introduced by varying user densities and content popularity on cache placement solutions. They developed an innovative multi-armed bandit approach to estimate user preferences in overlapping edge server regions, ensuring optimal cache placement. Similarly, **Li et al., (2021)** proposed a groundbreaking strategy combining universal coded caching with device computing. This approach aims to decrease average transmission bandwidth for virtual authenticity traffic while maintaining stringent QoS guarantees. a basic cloud caching approach is given in **Fig. 2.3**.

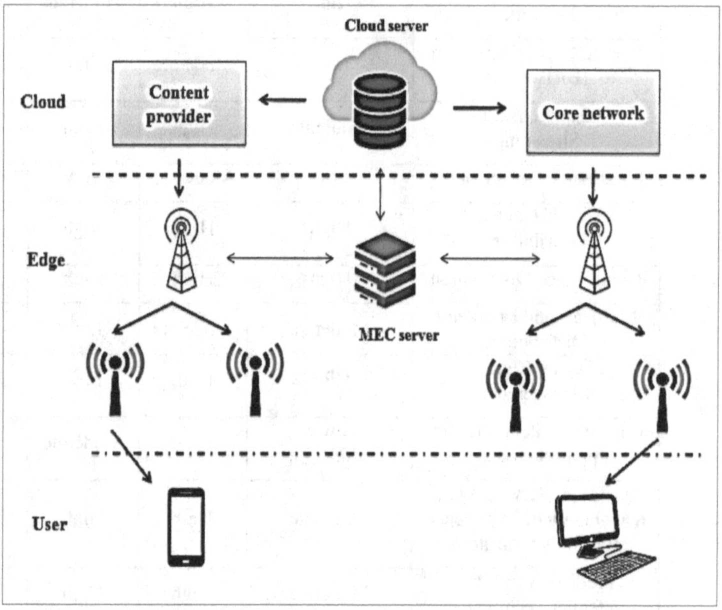

Fig. 2.3 Basic edge caching approach

Feng et al., (2021) constructed a two-tier MEC system that smartly integrates data caching and computing offloading. Their policy meticulously balances user costs by considering task offloading deadlines, AP cache capacities, and MEC server computing capabilities. Focusing on multi-bitrate video downloading within MEC networks, **Tran et al., (2017)** intended an ingenious cooperative caching and transcoding strategy named CoPro-CoCache. Utilizing the Least Recently Used caching strategy, videos are cached on servers until the space is exhausted. The transcoding tasks are dynamically allocated to the least loaded server, ensuring load balance across MEC servers. Enhancing user QoE,

Zhang et al., (2021) proposed an edge-assisted adaptive video downloading solution that marries super-resolution technology with edge caching. This integration elevates the quality of cached low-resolution videos at the edge. Further enhancing video streaming experiences, **Qiao et al., (2020)** studied an online ABR algorithm that seamlessly incorporates a user QoE perception interface and adaptive algorithm with elastic parameters, guaranteeing QoE diversity adaptation. **Tran et al., (2018)** examined an MEC-enhanced adaptive bit rate video distribution scheme based on the LRU strategy. This scheme is designed to decrease video transmission delays and enhance user QoE. Moreover, they developed a rate selection algorithm based on LBP for wireless access networks. This algorithm maximizes wireless network capacity by eliminating video stagnation under user QoE constraints.

Table 2.3 Comparison of Advanced Video Distribution Techniques

Technique	**Flexibility**	**Compatibility**	**Environment**	**Practical Execution**
Cloud and Edge Caching	High	High	Cloud and Edge	Complex
Multi-Armed Bandit Approach for Cache	High	Moderate	Edge	Moderate
Coded Caching with Device Computing	Moderate	High	Cloud and Edge	Moderate
Two-Tier MEC System	High	High	MEC	Complex
Cooperative Caching and Transcoding (CoPro-CoCache)	High	High	MEC	Complex
Edge-Assisted Adaptive Video Downloading	High	High	Edge	Complex
Online ABR Algorithm with QoE Perception	High	High	Edge	Moderate
MEC-Enhanced ABR Video Distribution	High	High	MEC	Complex
QoE-Driven Cache Placement Strategy	Moderate	High	Edge	Moderate

Lastly, **Li et al., (2017)** focused on QoE-driven cache placement strategies under initial delay constraints. Their approach aims to maximize average video distortion reduction, significantly enhancing the video downloading experience for users.

Table 2.3 confirmations the Comparison of Advanced Video Distribution Techniques on various metrics such as flexibility, compatibility, environment and practical execution.

2.7 Machine Learning in Caching Mechanisms

The rapid surge in video content downloading in current years has underscored the pressing need for advanced cache management resolutions to alleviate network congestion and enhance user practices globally. Traditional caching systems, which have long been integral to content delivery networks, are facing challenges due to the dynamic and impulsive nature of modern content consumption patterns (**Naeem et al., 2023**). Since 2019, research has increasingly focused on employing machine learning techniques to improve video caching strategies at the network edge. A basic ML embedded caching mecahnsim is illustrated in **Fig. 2.4**.

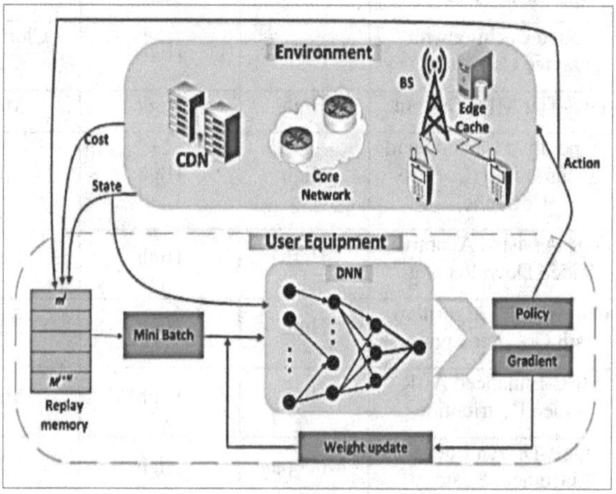

Fig. 2.4 ML embedded caching mechanism

2.7.1 Reinforcement Learning (RL)

Reinforcement learning offers a dynamic and adaptive approach to caching. RL algorithms can enhance network performance by continuously regulating caching strategies based on environmental feedback, marking a significant departure from the static nature of traditional tactics. This demonstrates RL potential to greatly enhance the efficiency and reliability of VoD services (**Dehury et al., 2023**). **Jiang et al., (2019)** demonstrated the use of Multi-Agent Reinforcement Learning (MARL) for cooperative content caching, utilizing historical data on content demand to predict user predilections. This method enhances cache hit rates and reduces content download delays, highlighting its practicality in mobile edge networks. **Sadeghi et al., (2018)** assumed a time-varying global content popularity profile modeled as a Markov chain. They employed Q-learning with linear approximation methods for scalable caching. **Qian et al., (2020)** and **Qiao et al., (2020)** assumed user demand and mobility follow Markov chains, respectively, and proposed hierarchical RL combining value function approximation Q-learning and deep Q-network (DQN) are used for assessing long-term popularity and short-term temporal correlation. **Majidi et al., (2022)** studied collaborative content caching in mobile devices, predicting user requests and grouping users for collaborative caching. They used a Q-learning approach in a coalesced setting to optimize the cooperative caching method.

Table 2.4 presents the association of various reinforcement learning techniques used for caching, highlighting the key techniques, assumptions, key metrics and environments.

These techniques aim to improve caching efficiency, scalability, and user experience by leveraging advanced algorithms and considering different environmental factors.

Table 2.4 Comparison of Various Reinforcement Learning Techniques

Technique	Key Techniques	Assumptions	Key Metrics	Environment
Dynamic and Adaptive Caching	RL algorithms	Environmental feedback	Enhanced efficiency and reliability	VoD services
Multi-Agent Reinforcement Learning	Cooperative content caching	Historical content demand	Increased cache hit rates, reduced content download delays	Mobile edge networks
Q-learning with Linear Approximation	Scalable caching	Time-varying global content popularity as a Markov chain	Scalability	General caching environments
Hierarchical Reinforcement Learning	Value function approximation Q-learning, DQN	User demand and mobility follow Markov chains	Long-term popularity, short-term temporal correlation	Various networks with dynamic user demands, mobile networks
Federated Q-learning for Collaborative Caching	Collaborative content caching	User request prediction, user grouping	Optimized collaborative caching, scalability	Mobile devices

2.7.2 Deep Reinforcement Learning (DRL)

Deep Reinforcement Learning is particularly compatible for the unpredictable dynamics of video caching, as it can knob high-dimensional state spaces by merging deep learning with RL **(Alipio et al., 2023)**. **Luo et al., (2020)** developed a mechanism combining edge caching, video transcoding, and transmission with DRL using the asynchronous advantage actor-critic (A3C) algorithm. This model exploits energy efficiency and enhances the quality of experience in video streaming. **Wang et al., (2020)** introduced FADE, a federated DRL framework for cooperative edge caching in IoT scenarios. This architecture allows base stations to collaboratively develop a common predictive model, significantly reducing performance degradation, average latency, and backhaul traffic while enhancing the hit rate. **Zhang et al., (2022)** developed a privacy-preserving Q-learning-based optimization framework called VC-PPQ for mobile edge networks. This system effectively balances user privacy with cache services, improving the video quality of experience (VQoE) for mobile users.

Table 2.5 presents a relationship of various Deep Reinforcement Learning techniques used for caching, highlighting the Practical Applications, assumptions, key metrics and environments.

Table 2.5 Comparison of Various Deep Reinforcement Learning Techniques

Technique	Practical Applications	Assumptions	Key Metrics	Environment
Deep Reinforcement Learning	Handling unpredictable video caching dynamics	Handles high-dimensional state spaces	Improved adaptability and learning efficiency	Video caching
A3C Algorithm for Edge Caching	Enhancing streaming quality and efficiency	Energy efficiency and quality of experience maximization	Enhanced quality of experience, energy efficiency	Video streaming
Federated DRL Framework	Cooperative caching for IoT scenarios	IoT scenarios, collaborative predictive modeling	Reduced latency, backhaul traffic, improved hit rate	IoT and edge networks
Privacy-Preserving Q-Learning	Enhancing VQoE while preserving user privacy	Balances user privacy with cache services	Improved video quality of experience	Mobile edge networks

2.7.3 Edge caching Approaches

Chen et al., (2020) projected a cooperative edge caching mechanism based on multi-agent DRL. They formulated the caching problem as a Partially Observable Markov Decision Process (POMDP)–based multi-agent decision problem, optimizing costs related with content retrieval from servers, content sharing among base stations (BSs), and content caching within local BSs. **Sun**

et al., (2023) proposed an edge caching approach using federated DRL, integrating edge caching and recommender systems to create a recommendation-enabled edge caching system in mobile edge-cloud computing networks. Their federated discrete soft actor–critic (FDSAC) algorithm incorporates LSTM to capture time-series dependencies of replacement activities. **Yang et al., (2022)** introduced a collaborative caching and transcoding approach for 360-degree video streaming using a deep deterministic policy gradient (DRL-CTCS) algorithm. This approach aims to reduce transmission costs, quality mismatch levels, and delays while adhering to cache storage and computation capacity limitations.

Table 2.6 illustrates a comparison of reinforcement learning techniques for edge caching based on studies.

Table 2.6 Comparison of Reinforcement Learning Techniques for Edge Caching

Study	Technique	Flexibility	Adaptability	Accuracy
Chen et al., (2020)	Multi-Agent DRL	High	Low	High
Sun et al., (2023)	Federated DRL	High	High	High
Yang et al., (2022)	DRL-CTCS	Moderate	High	High

2.7.4 Long Short-Term Memory (LSTM)

LSTM networks have been emphasized for their role in caching by enabling systems to learn about content popularity over various time intervals, leading to improved cache replacement policies. **Zhang et al., (2019)** introduced an LSTM-based edge-assisted intelligent caching framework called LSTM-C, which establishes cache replacement policies that outperform traditional methods in terms of cache hit rates. **Narayanan et al., (2018)** anticipated deep cache on the basis of the sequence-to-sequence LSTM model to predict user content requests. **Jiang et al., (2020)** used the k-nearest neighboring (KNN) algorithm to learn popularity trends and intended a deep learning-based caching method depending on possible trends. **Maniotis et al., (2020)** employed LSTM to predict subsequent content requests, proactively caching tiles and layers of expected videos encoded by SVC.

Conveying high-quality video content to a large and changing number of users remains challenging, even with advancements in VoD service architecture and increasingly sophisticated caching solutions. This challenge is especially pronounced during peak demand periods. Conventional caching systems primarily rely on fixed rules for storing and evicting items, such as the Least Recently Used or Least Frequently Used methods. These strategies face several challenges, including accurately predicting content popularity, maintaining consistent user experience, effectively managing resources, and competently handling the growing volume of content and users (**Niknam et al., 2020**).

Table 2.7 illustrates comparison of LSTM-based caching techniques and conventional caching systems based on adaptability, accuracy, Scalability and Efficiency.

Table 2.7 Comparison of LSTM-based Caching Techniques

Technique	Adaptability	Accuracy	Scalability	Efficiency
DeepCache	High	High	Moderate	High
KNN with deep learning	Moderate	High	Moderate	Moderate
LSTM for proactive caching	High	High	High	High
LSTM-C	High	High	High	High
Conventional caching methods	Low	Moderate	High	High

Table 2.8 indicates the detailed comparison of various machine learning techniques in caching mechanisms based on performance, implementation cost, accuracy and complexity.

Table 2.8 Comparison of various Machine Learning Techniques in Caching Mechanism

Technique	Performance	Implementation Cost	Accuracy	Complexity
Reinforcement Learning	High	Moderate	High	High
Deep Reinforcement Learning	Very High	High	Very High	Very High
Edge Caching Approaches	High	High	High	High
Long Short-Term Memory	High	Moderate	High	High

2.8 Video Optimization Techniques

Dynamic resolution adjustment in video streaming dynamically adapts the video resolution on the basis of the user's device screen size and existing network conditions. **Debevec et al., (2023)** commended that this approach optimizes the viewing experience by selecting the most suitable resolution in real-time. Algorithms detect the type of device accessing the video stream, considering factors like screen resolution and processing capabilities, while monitoring network speed to ensure smooth playback. By selecting the optimal resolution—ranging from high-definition to lower resolutions—according to available bandwidth, dynamic resolution adjustment minimizes buffering and maintains video quality. This adaptive strategy enhances user satisfaction by delivering seamless video playback across various devices and network environments, making it a pivotal feature in modern video streaming technologies.

Content-aware encoding is a sophisticated technique used in video processing to optimize encoding settings based on the specific characteristics of the content being encoded, such as high-motion versus static scenes (**Seeliger**

et al., 2022). The concept involves using machine learning algorithms to analyze video frames in real-time and dynamically adjust parameters like bitrates and compression settings. For instance, scenes with high motion or rapid changes may require higher bitrates to preserve quality and detail, whereas static scenes with little motion can be encoded more efficiently at lower bitrates to conserve bandwidth. This adaptive approach ensures that the video maintains optimal quality throughout playback, enhancing viewer experience across various viewing conditions.

Kua et al., (2017) suggested that Frame rate adaptation adjusts the frame rate of the video stream rendering to the content and prevailing network conditions. Lowering the frame rate during static or low-motion sequences helps reduce bandwidth consumption without significantly impacting visual quality. Conversely, increasing the frame rate for high-motion scenes enhances smoothness and detail, particularly beneficial for action-packed or fast-paced content. By dynamically adjusting frame rates, this technique optimizes streaming performance and maintains a consistent viewing experience across diverse network speeds and device capabilities.

Aspect ratio adaptation addresses the challenge of displaying videos across different screen sizes and orientations, such as landscape and portrait modes. This concept involves dynamically adjusting the aspect ratio of the video by cropping or padding the content as necessary to fit the viewer's screen dimensions seamlessly (**Caplan et al., 2020**). Implementing aspect ratio adaptation ensures that videos are displayed correctly and optimally on various devices, enhancing usability and visual appeal.

Thumbnail previews provide users with small, low-resolution snapshots of video segments to facilitate navigation and content selection. **Vermast et al., (2023)** commended that this concept involves extracting key frames from the video and displaying them as thumbnails, allowing users to preview the content without downloading the entire file. Thumbnail previews enable quick browsing and decision-making, enhancing user engagement and satisfaction by offering visual cues that aid in selecting desired video content efficiently. This feature is particularly useful in video-on-demand services and platforms where users browse through extensive libraries of content.

Table 2.9 illustrates the Comparison of various video optimization techniques based on different metrics such as user engagement, video quality, downloading speed and implementation cost.

Table 2.9 Comparison of various Video Optimization Techniques

Technique	User Engagement	Video Quality	Downloading Speed	Implementation Cost
Dynamic Resolution Adjustment	Enhances by providing seamless playback experiences.	Maintains optimal quality across devices and network speeds.	Improves by adapting resolution to prevent buffering.	Moderate
Content-aware Encoding	Increases by ensuring consistent high-quality playback.	Preserves quality by adjusting parameters dynamically.	Enhances with efficient encoding tailored to content.	High
Frame Rate Adaptation	Maintains by optimizing visual experience across networks.	Balances detail and smoothness based on scene dynamics.	Improves with efficient bandwidth utilization.	Low to moderate
Aspect Ratio Adaptation	Enhances usability across devices with seamless display.	Ensures correct display without distortion.	Facilitates faster loading with optimized aspect ratios.	Low to moderate
Thumbnail Previews	Improves engagement by facilitating quick browsing.	Aids in quick content selection with visual previews.	Reduces initial load times with preview capabilities.	Low

These metrics highlight how each technique contributes differently to optimizing video streaming, addressing aspects from quality preservation to user engagement, and considering practical factors such as implementation costs and download speeds.

2.9 Data Compression Techniques

2.9.1 Efficient Codecs

Efficient codecs are pivotal in video encoding, emphasizing superior compression capabilities while maintaining high quality. These codecs optimize data storage and transmission by reducing file sizes without compromising visual fidelity. H.265 (HEVC), recognized as High Efficiency Video Coding, signifies a notable advancement over its predecessor H.264, delivering substantial compression enhancements (**Pastuszak et al., 2015**). VP9, an open-source codec from Google, is renowned for its efficient compression tailored for web video, supporting high-resolution streaming with reduced bandwidth requirements. AV1, established by the Alliance for Open Media, represents the latest innovation in video compression technology. It promises superior compression efficiency compared to both H.265 and VP9, making it ideal for delivering high-quality video content across various platforms and devices. These codecs collectively enable more efficient video streaming, enhancing user experience through faster load times, smoother playback, and optimized bandwidth utilization. Their adoption continues to shape the landscape of digital video delivery, ensuring optimal performance in diverse streaming environments. An example of AI-based video compression using codecs is depicted in **Fig. 2.5**.

2.9.2 Transcoding

Transcoding is a crucial process in video content delivery that involves converting videos into different formats to balance between quality and file size, thereby optimizing download speeds and ensuring compatibility across various devices and network conditions. The concept of transcoding revolves around using specialized tools and algorithms to encode videos into multiple versions at different bitrates, resolutions, and formats (**Asakawa et al., 2019**). This approach enables adaptive streaming, where the video player dynamically switches between these versions on the basis of user's network bandwidth and device capabilities.

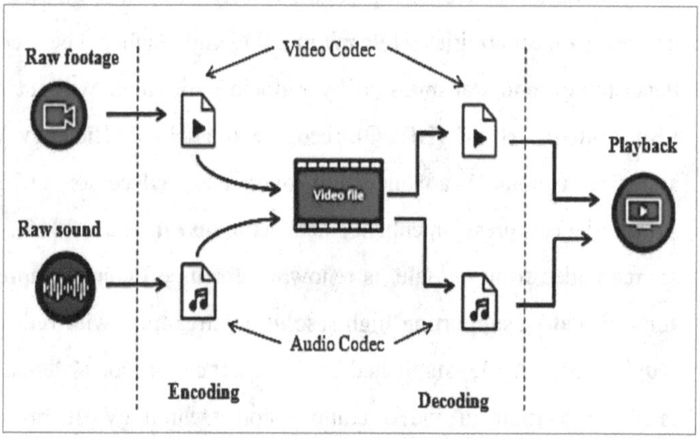

Fig. 2.5 AI-based video compression using codecs

2.9.3 Lossless and Lossy Compression

In digital data management, two primary compression methods, lossless and lossy, play critical roles in balancing file size reduction with preserving quality. **Mentzer et al., (2020)** anticipated that Lossless compression reduces file sizes without any data loss, maintaining the original data integrity, which is crucial for applications like archival storage and professional editing where every detail must be preserved. Conversely, lossy compression achieves higher compression rates by selectively discarding some data, which can lead to a perceptible loss in quality compared to the origina**l.,** This method is commonly employed in streaming media and other applications where reducing file size is prioritized over maintaining absolute fidelity. The choice between lossless and lossy compression depends on the explicit requirements of the use case, ensuring optimal performance in storage efficiency, transmission bandwidth, and overall user experience across diverse digital environments.

2.9.4 Entropy Coding

Entropy coding employs sophisticated techniques like Huffman coding, arithmetic coding, and context-adaptive binary arithmetic coding (CABAC) to enhance the efficiency of video data compression. These methods capitalize on statistical properties of data to reduce redundancy and achieve higher compression rates within video codecs (**Cui et al., 2016**). Huffman coding, for instance, allocates shorter codes to frequently occurring symbols in the data, effectively minimizing the average length of the encoded bit stream. Arithmetic coding takes this further by encoding entire sequences of symbols into fractional values, thereby achieving even greater compression ratios by using a single floating-point number to represent categorization of symbols. Context-adaptive binary arithmetic coding (CABAC) adapts its coding process based on the probability dissemination of symbols in the current context, further optimizing compression based on local patterns within the data. Implementing these advanced entropy coding techniques within video codecs significantly enhances compression efficiency, leading to reduced file sizes without compromising perceptual quality, thus playing a critical role in modern digital video processing and distribution systems (**Auli-Llinas et al., 2015**).

Table 2.10 shows the comparison of various data compression techniques. Each of these techniques has its strengths and ideal use cases, depending on whether the priority is on file size, quality, compatibility, or efficiency.

Each of these techniques offers unique benefits and trade-offs, making them suitable for different use cases depending on the need for file size reduction, quality maintenance, or compatibility across devices.

Table 2.10 Comparison of Data Compression Techniques

Technique	Description	Example Codecs / Methods
Efficient Codecs	Focuses on high-quality video compression while reducing file sizes.	H.265 (HEVC), VP9, AV1
Transcoding	Converts videos into different formats and resolutions to optimize download speeds and device compatibility.	Tools and algorithms for adaptive streaming
Lossless Compression	Reduces file size without losing data, maintaining original quality.	Used for archival storage, professional editing
Lossy Compression	Achieves higher compression rates by discarding some data, compromising quality for reduced file sizes.	Common in streaming media
Entropy Coding	Enhances compression efficiency using techniques like Huffman coding, arithmetic coding, and CABAC.	Huffman coding, arithmetic coding, CABAC

2.10 Optimized Delivery Protocols

Herrero et al., (2020) acclaimed that QUIC (Quick UDP Internet Connections) represents a significant advancement in internet transport protocols, developed by Google to optimize connection speed and efficiency by leveraging User Datagram Protocol (UDP) instead of old-fashioned Transmission Control Protocol (TCP). This protocol integrates connection establishment and encryption mechanisms directly, drastically reducing latency during initial connection setups compared to TCP. The key advantages of QUIC include its ability to establish connections faster, support multiplexing of numerous data streams over a solitary connection without head-of-line blocking, and implement superior congestion control algorithms that adapt swiftly to network conditions. By enabling QUIC on both server and client sides, organizations can capitalize on its performance benefits, ensuring quicker data transmission and enhanced user experience across a wide range of applications, particularly those necessitating real-time interaction like video streaming and online gaming.

Web Real-Time Communication (WebRTC) revolutionizes digital communication by enabling direct, plugin-free audio and video interactions amongst web browsers and devices. This technology facilitates seamless real-time communication experiences like video conferencing, voice calls, and lives streaming by leveraging standardized APIs integrated into web browsers (**Kim et al., 2020**). WebRTC's primary advantage lies in its ability to establish low-latency peer-to-peer connections, minimizing delays and enhancing responsiveness for applications requiring immediate interaction. Moreover, it supports scalability by reducing server load through direct user-to-user communication, making it suitable for services handling numerous simultaneous connections efficiently. Implementing WebRTC involves integrating its JavaScript APIs into web and mobile applications, empowering developers to incorporate features like video conferencing and collaborative browsing directly within their platforms. By embracing WebRTC, organizations can optimize user engagement, streamline communication processes, and deliver robust real-time communication solutions across various digital environments. **Fig. 2.6** gives the framework of WebRTC.

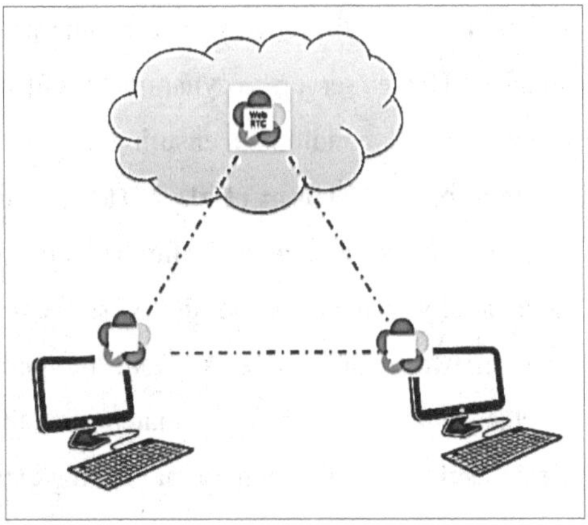

Fig. 2.6 Framework of WebRTC

HTTP/2 and HTTP/3 represent significant advancements in the HTTP protocol aimed at improving performance, especially in the realm of video streaming and content delivery. HTTP/2 introduces features like multiplexing, allowing manifold requests and responses to be transmitted concurrently over a solitary TCP connection. This capability reduces latency and enhances throughput by efficiently utilizing network resources. Additionally, **Belshe et al., (2015)** proposed that HTTP/2 incorporates header compression to minimize overhead, further optimizing data transmission efficiency. Building on these improvements, HTTP/3 adopts the QUIC protocol instead of TCP, leveraging its benefits such as reduced connection setup times and improved congestion control. By combining HTTP/2's multiplexing and header compression with QUIC's low-latency capabilities, HTTP/3 enhances the responsiveness and reliability of web communication (**Chatzoglou et al., 2023**). To harness these enhancements, it is essential for both web servers and clients to support HTTP/2 and HTTP/3 protocols, ensuring streamlined content delivery and superior user experience across diverse digital environments.

MPEG-DASH (Dynamic Adaptive Streaming over HTTP) and HLS (HTTP Live Streaming) are leading adaptive bitrate streaming protocols designed to optimize media delivery over the internet. MPEG-DASH leverages conventional HTTP web servers to dynamically adjust video quality on the basis of real-time network conditions, ensuring smooth playback and reducing buffering interruptions (**Niamut et al., 2016**). Similarly, HLS, established by Apple, segments video content into slighter parts that can be delivered and played sequentially, enhancing flexibility and compatibility across various devices and network environments. Both protocols excel in adaptability, adjusting video quality on-the-fly to match available bandwidth and device capabilities, thereby providing consistent viewing experiences. **Bentaleb et al., (2022)** advised that implementation involves encoding and packaging video content into either DASH or HLS formats using compatible tools, and deploying these formats with supported players for seamless playback. By adopting MPEG-DASH or HLS, content providers can deliver reliable, high-quality streaming experiences that cater to diverse user preferences and network conditions, enhancing overall viewer satisfaction in digital media consumption scenarios.

A comparative analysis of QUIC, WebRTC, HTTP/2, HTTP/3, MPEG-DASH, and HLS based on metrics such as performance, implementation cost, accuracy, and reliability is presented in **Table 2.11**.

Table 2.11 Comparative Analysis of Optimized Delivery Protocols

Techniques	Performance	Implementation Cost	Accuracy	Reliability
QUIC	QUIC excels in speed and efficiency, with faster connection setups, multiplexing capabilities, and superior congestion control.	Moderate	High	Offers robust connection resilience and effective congestion management.
WebRTC	Offers robust connection resilience and effective congestion management	Low	High	Resilient to network fluctuations, stable peer connections
HTTP/2	Enhances data transmission efficiency with multiplexing and header compression	Moderate	High	Ensures reliable data transmission and reduced overhead
HTTP/3	Builds on HTTP/2 features with improved latency and congestion control using QUIC	Moderate	High	Improved reliability with reduced latency and efficient congestion handling
MPEG-DASH	Enthusiastically adjusts video quality based on network conditions, reducing buffering	Low	High	Stable delivery over HTTP, reducing interruptions
HLS	Segments video content for flexible streaming across devices	Low	High	Stable delivery over HTTP, suitable for diverse network environments

2.11 Video Content Downloading Algorithms

These algorithms are designed to progress the efficiency and quality of video content delivery over networks. Here's an overview and some thoughts on each:

(A) Adaptive Mesh-based Streaming (AMS) Algorithm

Audet et al., (2019) projected the Adaptive Mesh-based Streaming algorithm as a sophisticated approach designed to enthusiastically adjust streaming quality on the basis of real-time network conditions. Unlike traditional streaming methods, AMS employs a mesh network topology, where each node in the network can connect to multiple other nodes. This connectivity allows for the optimization of delivery paths, significantly plummeting latency and improving the overall quality of services.

AMS proves to be highly effective in environments characterized by fluctuating network conditions due to its ability to adapt in real-time (**Abbas et al., 2020**). The use of a mesh network approach not only provides redundancy but also enhances the reliability and resilience of the system against node failures. This redundancy ensures that even if one node fails, the data can still be delivered through alternative paths, maintaining the continuity and quality of the streaming service. However, the complexity associated with managing and maintaining a mesh network can be a notable drawback.

Compared to simpler topologies, a mesh network requires more sophisticated algorithms and infrastructure to ensure optimal performance and stability. Despite this complexity, the benefits of AMS in terms of adaptability, reliability, and improved QoS make it a valuable approach for modern streaming applications, especially in scenarios where network conditions are unpredictable and highly variable.

(B) Hybrid Proxy-aided Streaming (HPS) Algorithm

The Hybrid Proxy-aided Streaming algorithm combines the use of proxies with direct client-server communication to optimize streaming. In this approach, proxies act as intermediaries that cache content, which diminishes the load on the main server and improves delivery speed (**Fursov et al., 2020**). By serving content from the nearest proxy, HPS can balance the load and reduce latency, enhancing the overall streaming performance.

This algorithm is particularly advantageous in high-traffic scenarios, as it offloads the server and distributes the load across multiple proxies. This distribution can significantly improve the user experience by reducing buffering times and providing faster access to content. However, the primary challenge with HPS lies in the efficient management of proxy caches to ensure they store the most relevant and frequently accessed content. Efficient cache management is crucial for maintaining the system's performance and optimizing content delivery.

(C) Randomized Chunk Selection (RCS) Algorithm

The Randomized Chunk Selection algorithm randomly selects chunks of video content to download, rather than following a sequential order. This approach helps avoid network congestion and ensures a more uniform distribution of data traffic. **Chapuis et al., (2016)** stated that by randomizing chunk selection, RCS can reduce the chances of bottlenecks and improve the robustness of streaming. It is particularly effective in peer-to-peer (P2P) networks, where multiple sources can provide the chunks, thus balancing the load across different parts of the network and making the overall system more efficient.

However, a potential downside of RCS is the increased initial buffering time, as critical chunks needed for playback might not be downloaded first, potentially delaying the start of video playback.

(D) Dynamic Adaptive Streaming over HTTP (DASH)

Dynamic Adaptive Streaming over HTTP (DASH), also identified as MPEG-DASH, is ordinary for streaming video over the internet. It works by breaking the content into small segments, each encoded at different bitrates. The client animatedly selects the suitable segment on the basis of current network conditions, device capabilities, and user preferences.

Bentaleb et al., (2018) suggested that DASH is widely adopted due to its flexibility and adaptability, providing a good balance between quality and buffering by adjusting in real-time to changes in network conditions. However, its performance depends heavily on the accuracy of network condition estimation, as inaccurate estimations can lead to suboptimal segment selection and affect the streaming experience.

(E) Scalable Video Coding (SVC)

Scalable Video Coding is an addition of the H.264/MPEG-4 AVC video compression standard. It permits the encoding of a high-quality video stream with several subset streams that can be decoded at lower quality (Nasrabadi et al., 2017). This feature allows for adaptation to diverse network conditions and device capabilities without the need for multiple encodings. SVC is efficient for delivering video to a wide variety of devices through varying capabilities, supporting real-time adaptation and reducing the need for extensive storage. However, the complexity in encoding and decoding SVC streams can be higher compared to non-scalable codecs, posing a challenge in implementation. Benefits of SVC are Efficiency, Adaptability and Compatibility.

(F) BitTorrent-Based Streaming

Hammami et al., (2015) argued that BitTorrent-based streaming leverages the BitTorrent protocol for video distribution. Instead of downloading a file sequentially, the video is divided into chunks that can be downloaded from multiple peers simultaneously. Examples of this approach include platforms like Popcorn Time. This method is highly scalable and can efficiently handle enormous numbers of users, decreasing the load on dominant servers and providing high download speeds. However, it may face legal and copyright challenges, and initial buffering can be an issue due to the distributed nature of the downloading process.

(G) Patching Multicast

Patching multicast is a technique employed in IPTV and other video streaming services. When a new client joins a live stream, it initially receives a unicast patch stream to catch up to the current broadcast. After catching up, the client switches to the multicast stream. This method is efficient for live streaming and reduces server load, ensuring new clients quickly catch up to the live broadcast without long delays **(Akbar et al., 2017)**. However, the implementation complexity and the necessity for real-time synchronization pose significant encounters.

(H) Forward Error Correction (FEC)

Forward Error Correction (FEC) is a technique accustomed to improve data reliability by accumulating redundant data to the video stream. This permits the receiver to perceive and spot the errors without needing retransmissions, making it particularly useful in environments with high packet loss. **Blawat et al., (2016)** advocated that FEC improves the quality of streaming in unreliable network conditions, reducing the need for retransmissions, which can save bandwidth and reduce latency. Nevertheless, the trade-off is additional overhead and improved computational complexity, which can impact performance and resource utilization. Benefits of FEC are Error Correction, Efficiency and Bandwidth Saving

Each of these algorithms and techniques addresses specific challenges in video content downloading, such as scalability, adaptability, reliability, and user experience. The choice of algorithm depends on factors like network conditions, device capabilities, content type, and user expectations.

Table 2.12 Comparison of Various Video Content Downloading Algorithms

Algorithm	Scalability	Adaptability	Reliability	User Experience
Dynamic Adaptive Streaming over HTTP	High	High	Moderate to High	High
Scalable Video Coding	Moderate to High	High	High	High
BitTorrent-Based Streaming	Very High	Moderate	Moderate to High	Moderate to High
Patching Multicast	Moderate to High	Moderate	High	Moderate to High
Forward Error Correction	Moderate	Low to Moderate	High	Moderate
Adaptive Mesh-based Streaming	High	High	High	High
Hybrid Proxy-aided Streaming	High	Moderate	High	High
Randomized Chunk Selection	High	Moderate	Moderate to High	Moderate

Table 2.12 shows the comparison of various video content downloading algorithms on various metrics such as scalability, adaptability, reliability and user experience.

2.12 Machine Learning-Based Data Distribution Algorithms For Video Content Downloading

Machine learning-based algorithms for data distribution and video content downloading are being explored to optimize performance, enhance user experience, and improve efficiency (**Tanzil et al., 2017**). Here are some examples of such algorithms for both general video content downloading and cloud-based video downloading:

Wei et al., (2021) proposed Reinforcement Learning for Adaptive Streaming (RLAS) leverages advanced machine learning techniques to dynamically adjust video quality in response to changing network conditions and user inclinations. By employing reinforcement learning, the algorithm continually interacts with its environment, learning optimal streaming strategies that enhance user experience by minimizing buffering and maximizing video quality. RLAS excels in scalability, capable of adapting to diverse network conditions and user behaviors through its training process. Its adaptability is exceptional, allowing for real-time adjustments based on learned policies, ensuring a reliable and uninterrupted streaming experience. Overall, RLAS stands out in providing a high-quality user experience characterized by seamless video streaming with minimal disruptions. **Fig. 2.7** represents the RLAS framework.

Deep Learning for Bandwidth Prediction (DLBP) employs sophisticated deep learning models to forecast available bandwidth by analyzing historical network data. These predictions are crucial for preemptively buffering and adjusting video quality to prevent congestion-related interruptions. DLBP boasts high scalability, effectively managing extensive datasets and intricate network patterns. Its adaptability is notable, continuously refining predictions with updated data to maintain accuracy (**Hatem et al., 2019**). With reliable bandwidth forecasts, DLBP significantly minimizes buffering risks, thereby enhancing user experience through consistently smooth video playback, proactively aligned with prevailing network conditions.

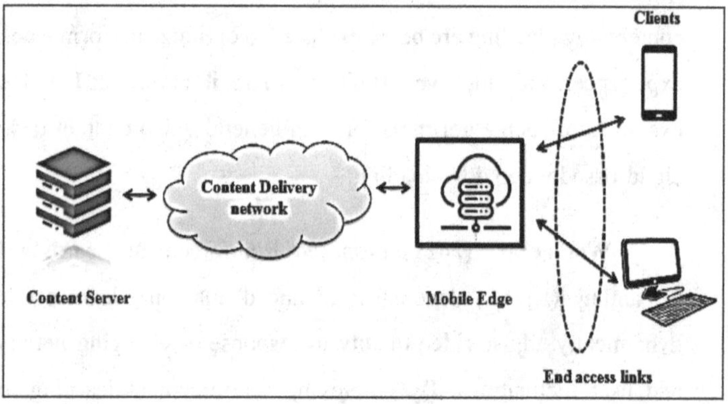

Fig. 2.7 RLAS framework

Yeh et al., (2020) suggested Collaborative Filtering for P2P Networks (CF-P2P) leverages collaborative filtering techniques to optimize the selection of peers within peer-to-peer streaming networks. By analyzing past interactions and performance metrics, CF-P2P enhances the efficiency of data distribution among peers. The algorithm exhibits high scalability, effectively managing increased numbers of peers and data points within the network. While its adaptability relies on historical data, which may not always reflect real-time conditions, CF-P2P offers moderate to high reliability depending on the accuracy of peer performance metrics. This approach significantly improves user experience by reducing latency and buffering through improved peer selection, ensuring smoother and more consistent streaming experiences for users.

Table 2.13 provides a comparative view of how RLAS, DLBP, and CF-P2P perform across various metrics such as dynamic adjustment, technique used, adaptability, reliability, user experience, and training complexity. Each algorithm offers unique strengths tailored to optimize performance and enhance user satisfaction in different aspects of video content downloading and distribution.

Table 2.13 Comparison of Various Machine Learning-Based Algorithms

Algorithm / Metric	**Reinforcement Learning for Adaptive Streaming (RLAS)**	**Deep Learning for Bandwidth Prediction (DLBP)**	**Collaborative Filtering for P2P Networks (CF-P2P)**
Dynamic Adjustment	Adjusts video quality based on network conditions and user preferences	Preemptively adjusts video quality based on predicted bandwidth	Optimizes peer selection for efficient data distribution
Technique Used	Reinforcement Learning	Deep Learning	Collaborative Filtering
Adaptability	Exceptional	Notable	Moderate to High
Reliability	High	High	Moderate to High
User Experience	Seamless streaming with minimal disruptions	Consistently smooth playback with reduced buffering	Reduced latency and buffering, smoother streaming
Training Complexity	Complex	Complex	Moderate

Resource Allocation using Machine Learning (RA-ML)utilizes machine learning models to accurately predict demand and efficiently allocate cloud resources, optimizing server capacity and load balancing for effective video content delivery **(Wang et al., 2019)**

2.13 Machine Learning-Based Algorithms For Cloud-Based Video Downloading

Resource Allocation using Machine Learning (RA-ML) utilizes machine learning models to accurately predict demand and efficiently allocate cloud resources, optimizing server capacity and load balancing for effective video content delivery (**Wang et al., 2019**). It boasts very high scalability by leveraging cloud infrastructure and machine learning capabilities, while its high adaptability ensures continuous updates based on demand patterns. RA-ML achieves very high reliability by preemptively allocating resources, minimizing service disruptions and ensuring a high-quality user experience with quick and reliable access to video content.

Narayanan et al., (2018) anticipated Content Caching using Neural Networks (CC-NN) implements neural networks to forecast popular content and strategically cache it closer to end-users, thereby reducing latency and server load. Its high scalability allows it to handle large datasets and predict caching needs effectively, while maintaining high adaptability by adjusting to evolving content popularity trends. CC-NN ensures high reliability through predictive caching, mitigating the risk of content unavailability and enhancing user experience by providing faster access to frequently accessed content.

Intelligent Data Routing (IDR) using ML employs machine learning algorithms to optimize data routing paths within cloud networks, minimizing latency and improving download speeds for efficient data flow. With high scalability suitable for large-scale cloud infrastructures, IDR adapts dynamically to changing network conditions, ensuring high reliability and consistent performance through intelligent routing strategies. This system significantly enhances user experience by delivering improved download speeds and reducing buffering interruptions (**Oloduowo et al., 2016**).

Table 2.14 highlights the strengths and focus areas of each algorithm: RA-ML focuses on demand prediction and resource allocation for server optimization; CC-NN emphasizes caching to reduce latency and server load; IDR optimizes data routing paths for improved download speeds and reduced buffering. Each system leverages machine learning to enhance performance, reliability, and user experience in different aspects of video content delivery and network optimization.

Table 2.14 Comparison of RA-ML, CC-NN, and IDR

Algorithm / Metric	RA-ML	CC-NN	IDR
Primary Function	Demand prediction, resource allocation	Content caching optimization	Data routing optimization
Reliability	Very High	High	High
User Experience	Quick and reliable access to video content	Faster access to popular content	Improved download speeds, reduced buffering
Data Utilization	Demand patterns, resource usage	Content popularity trends, caching needs	Network conditions, traffic patterns
Training Complexity	Moderate to Complex	Complex	Moderate to Complex
Scalability	Very High	High	High

2.14 Conclusion

The chapter begins by exploring methods to optimize P2P video downloading, emphasizing balanced overlay networks, incentive schemes, call admission control, and greedy algorithms for topology construction. These methods aim to ensure sufficient bandwidth allocation, enhance download rates, and maintain video downloading quality. The chapter also addresses cloud-based video content downloading constraints, focusing on cost management, performance issues, security concerns, and the need for scalable and efficient content delivery. Further, the chapter discusses Eye OS architecture, which integrates cloud storage, content delivery networks, edge computing, and adaptive streaming technologies to enhance video content management and delivery. Various video content distribution techniques, such as CDN, P2P distribution, adaptive bitrate streaming, and secure streaming protocols, are reviewed for their role in optimizing performance and user experience. Additionally, the chapter delves into caching mechanisms and the substantial impact of machine learning, including reinforcement learning, deep reinforcement learning, and LSTM networks, in enhancing caching efficiency and user experience in video content downloading.

Further, it explores advanced techniques and algorithms aimed at optimizing video streaming and downloading processes across diverse network environments and devices. It begins by detailing various video optimization strategies such as dynamic resolution adjustment, content-aware encoding, and frame rate adaptation to ensure high quality and efficient compression. The review also examines cutting-edge data compression techniques including efficient codecs like H.265 (HEVC) and VP9, and transcoding methods to optimize compatibility and download speeds. Optimized delivery protocols such as QUIC, WebRTC, and HTTP/3 are discussed for their roles in reducing latency and enhancing performance in real-time applications.

The review further delves into video content downloading algorithms like Adaptive Mesh-based Streaming and Hybrid Proxy-aided Streaming, highlighting their capabilities in adaptive streaming and load balancing. Methods to optimize P2P video downloading, such as balanced overlay networks and incentive schemes, are explored alongside considerations for cloud-based video content delivery, addressing cost management, security, and scalability. The integration of Eye OS architecture, combining cloud storage, CDN, edge computing, and adaptive streaming technologies, is emphasized for its role in enhancing video content management and delivery efficiency. Various distribution techniques including CDN, P2P distribution, and adaptive bitrate streaming are analyzed for their impact on performance and user experience. Finally, this chapter discusses caching mechanisms and the substantial influence of machine learning, including reinforcement learning and LSTM networks, in optimizing caching efficiency and augmenting user experience in video content downloading.

CHAPTER 3

Adaptive Cloud Downloads

3.1 Introduction

This chapter explores the cloud OS-based EAMS algorithm, covering its implementation and evaluation results.

3.2 System Architecture of EAMS Algorithm

This section delivers an overview of the system architecture for the EAMS algorithm.

(A) Cloud-based surrounding utilizing Eye OS

A cloud operating system denotes a computing platform that exists on a network, providing a comprehensive suite of applications accessible remotely. There are instances where having a dedicated cloud operating system is beneficial., Initially, when creating an account with the cloud OS, often available during special promotions such as the one-third anniversary event, users may encounter limitations. These limitations include restricted storage space and reliance on shared servers managed by various entities. The system performance and availability can be influenced by active users at any specified time. For those requiring a fanatical web operating system to manage data online and promote collaboration with colleagues or partners, establishing a personalized cloud environment becomes essential, By utilizing the Eye operating system, users can streamline tasks such as video downloads through cloud-based processes, enhancing efficiency and productivity.

(B) Video upload and segmentation

Colleagues openly upload videos to the cloud server, where they are segmented into specific fragments. Each segment, or block, is recognized by an output number allocated by the content server after excruciating. The encrypted block combination data, known as a link, is included in the meeting report. This link is a crucial 2D element to incorporate. It is essential to choose the correct byte length for each block, as it significantly impacts the system's performance. Each peer is part of an overlay community, and all peers are familiar with the community's structure.

(C) Manifold cache strategy

Numerous caches are employed by cloud server to streamline the file demand procedure in this phase. It receives download requests from all peers, and the cache distribution mechanism is determined on the basis of the current grade of every cache. To handle these requests, three cache storages are used in the proposed system. Each cache contains diverse sets of data, which are periodically refreshed from the cloud server. The status of each cache is categorized as either idle or busy, as illustrated in **Fig. 3.1**.

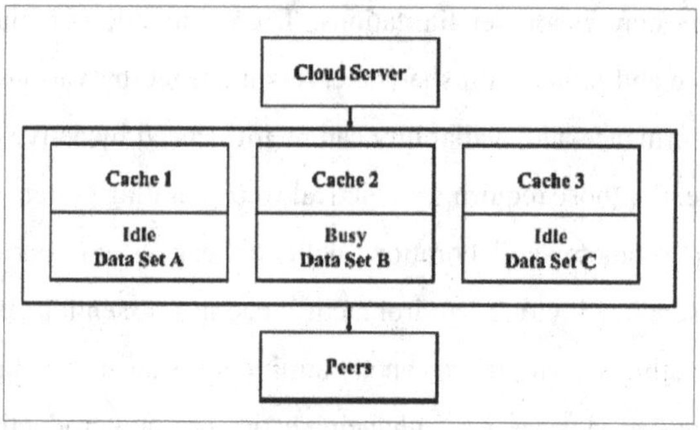

Fig. 3.1 Manifold cache strategy

3.3 Implementation of Enhanced Automated Mode Selection Algorithm

The module describes how to use a cloud server to deploy two modes: assistant mode and server mode. Furthermore, it employs an Advanced Adaptive Mode Selection (EAMS) rule set, allowing mechanical mode switching to improve server throughput and adaptability to the environment. The more sophisticated AMS rule set model covered in this article is represented by EAMS. Through extensive simulations, its ability to distribute accurate global performance in cloud mode has been validated. For choosing between server mode and assistant mode, EAMS provides an adaptable set of rules. Server mode and master mode each have specific benefits and drawbacks.

While server mode may use bandwidth from blocked contacts, the assistant mode makes use of peer-to-peer support as cloud servers continuously upload new content to help users' contacts. Every now and then, the cloud server modifies how each video is selected by running a complex set of automatic mode selection rules. For example, it forecasts L1's known charge. In the Cloud Garage, videos in assistant mode are given priority for coverage. As seen in **Fig. 3.2**, this prioritizing cuts down on preparation time by enabling larger users to contribute more storage by changing their status from lending to downloading. In this context, κ is a subset of movies cached via cloud storage. Ni denotes the number of peers for video j, U is the complement capacity of the peer, H is the full complement capacity of the cloud server Ni is the expected number of peers to be served over cloud, αj is the chance that the cloud server can help any peer to search video Nj through the most efficient single bite capture and K is the cache movie variety. Cu refers to Buffers and I commend multiple cache types.

The EAMS algorithm's flow chart, which dynamically switches between server and assistant mode depending on how many peers are requesting blocked videos, is shown in **Fig. 3.2**. The process begins by determining whether the number of active videos is less than a predefined threshold k.

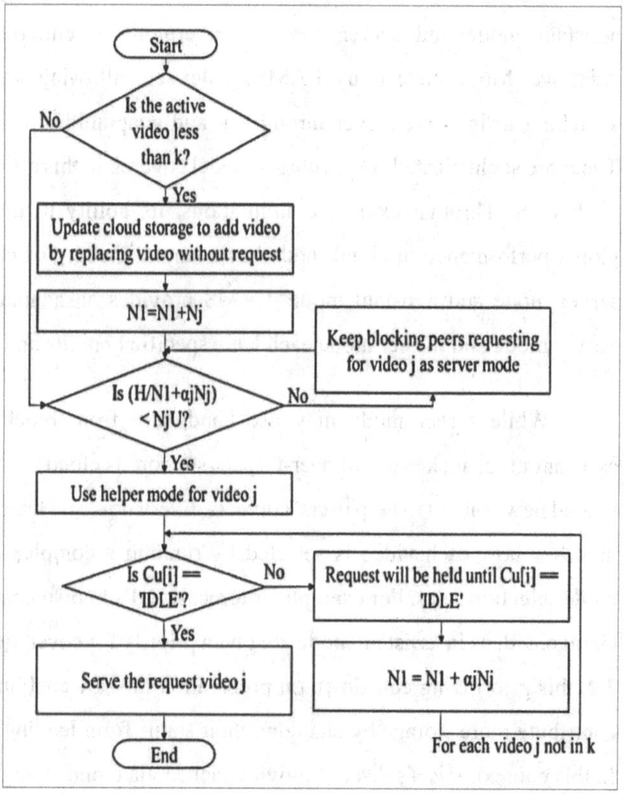

Fig. 3.2 Flow chart of the EAMS Algorithm

If it is not, the process loops back to continue checking. If the number of active videos is less than k, the cloud storage is updated by adding the requested video, potentially replacing a video that has no active requests. This triggers the calculation of the new video count N1, which is updated to N1=N1+Nj, where Nj represents the count of the newly added video.

Next, the system checks if the ratio is less than NjU, where H is a certain value related to system load, and αj is a coefficient. If this condition is not met, peers requesting video j are blocked, and the process continues in server mode. If the condition is satisfied, the system switches to a helper mode for video j.

Following this, the system checks if the state Cu[i] of the video is 'IDLE' or not. If it is not, the request is held until the video state becomes 'IDLE'. Once the video is idle, the video request is served, and the process ends. This operation ensures an optimized and balanced approach to serving video requests, managing system load, and efficiently handling video resources.

3.4 EAMS Algorithm

EAMS Algorithm used in the proposed system is as follows:

Algorithm 1: EAMS Algorithm

Input: κ, K, N_i, N_j, α_j, U, H, *Cu[i]*
Output: Updated cloud storage, status of video requests
Step 1: Initialize for every video j not in κ,
Step 2: Do if the active video is less than K than
Step 3: Update cloud storage to add video by replacing video without request.
N1=N1+Nj
Else
If (H/N1+αj Nj) <NjU then Use helper mode for video j If (Cu[i]=='IDLE') then
Step 4: Serve the request video jelse Cu[i]=='BUSY' then Request will be hold until Cu[i]=='IDLE'
N1 = N1 + αjNj
Else
Step 5: Keep blocking peers requesting for video j as server mode End if
End if

3.5 Results and Discussion

According to **Table 3.1**, the suggested EAMS algorithm is equivalent to the Adaptive Mesh-based Streaming, Hybrid Proxy-aided Streaming, and Randomized Chunk Selection (RCS) algorithms in terms of download time for different data speeds of 1, 2, 5, and 10 Mbps. Assuming perfect server load and network conditions, a sample 5-minute video with a 150 MB file size is used for this comparison.

Table 3.1 Comparison of download time of the suggested and state-of-art algorithms

Data Speed	AMS algorithm (Adaptive Mesh-based Streaming)	HPS algorithm (Hybrid Proxy-aided Streaming)	RCS algorithm (Randomized Chunk Selection)	EAMS algorithm (Enhanced Adaptive Mode Selection)
1 Mbps	03:00 min	02:30 min	02:45 min	02:15 min
2 Mbps	01:30 min	01:15 min	01:20 min	01:00 min
5 Mbps	00:36 min	00:30 min	00:32 min	00:24 min
10 Mbps	00:18 min	00:15 min	00:16 min	00:12 min

Table 3.2 Bandwidth for diverse Data Speeds and Download Modes

Data Speed and Download Mode	Bandwidth (Mbps)
1 Mbps Server	1 Mbps
1 Mbps P2P	2 Mbps
2 Mbps Server	2 Mbps
2 Mbps P2P	3 Mbps
5 Mbps Server	3 Mbps
5 Mbps P2P	4 Mbps
10 Mbps Server	6 Mbps
10 Mbps P2P	8 Mbps

A video's download time varies depending on the bandwidth that is available and the internet connection's speed. The bandwidth comparison for various data speeds and download modes is displayed in **Fig. 3.3**. Whereas **Table 3.2** shows the bandwidths corresponding to different data speeds and download modes, comparing server-based and peer-to-peer approaches.

Fig. 3.4 displays download times for different downloading modes namely, server and peer-to-peer—to determine which mode is faster under varying data speeds, real-time server loads, and network conditions. While.

Table 3.3 shows the download time corresponding to different data speeds and download modes comparing server-based and peer-to-peer approaches.

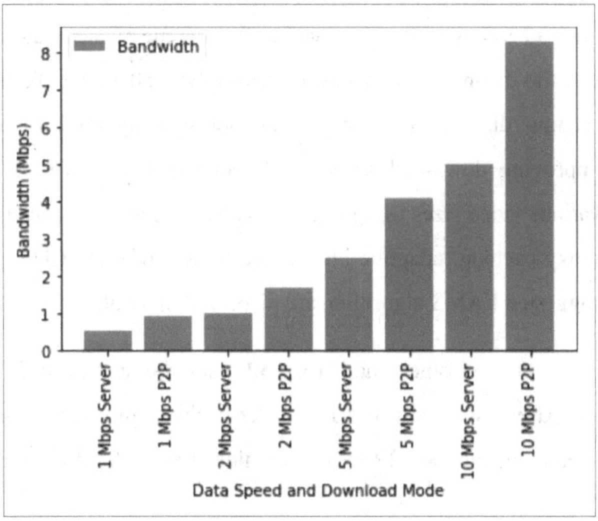

Fig. 3.3 Assessment of Bandwidth for diverse Data Speeds and Download modes

Table 3.3 Download Time for diverse Data Speeds and Download Modes

Data Speed and Download Mode	Download Time (seconds)
1 Mbps Server	5000
1 Mbps P2P	3000
2 Mbps Server	2500
2 Mbps P2P	1500
5 Mbps Server	1000
5 Mbps P2P	800
10 Mbps Server	500
10 Mbps P2P	300

Based on numerous tests, the optimal strategy for this video content downloading system is an arrangement of peer-to-peer and content distribution network caching. P2P enhances scalability and service capacity by distributing the load among peers. However, as the volume of user requests grows, ensuring fast file downloads becomes increasingly challenging. To mitigate this, CDN caching distributes video content across geographically dispersed servers, improving download speeds and reducing latency.The download times for various video sizes using different caching techniques, such as buffer caching, proxy caching, adaptive bitrate streaming, and P2P+CDN caching, using the suggested EAMS algorithm, are displayed in **Table 3.4**.

On the other hand, **Fig. 3.5** uses the suggested EAMS algorithm to compare download times for buffer caching, proxy caching, adaptive bitrate streaming, and the P2P + CDN caching strategy for different video sizes.

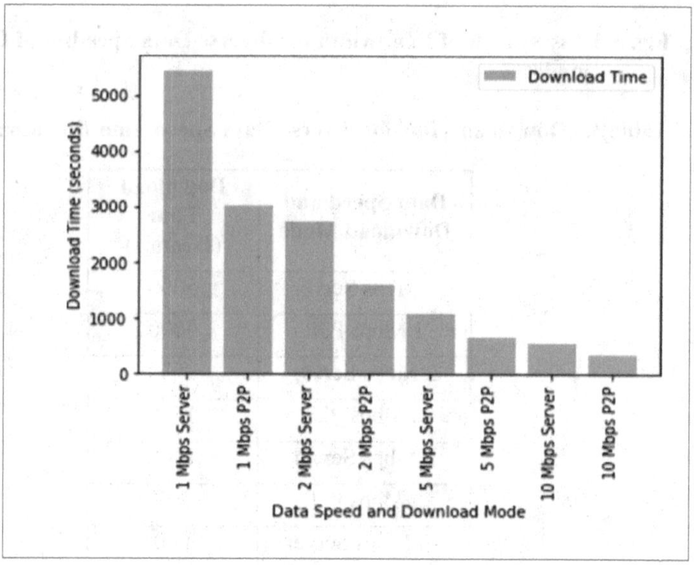

Fig. 3.4 Download Time for diverse Data Speeds and Download

Table 3.4 Download Time for diverse Video Sizes and Caching Methods

Video Size (MB)	Buffer Caching (s)	Proxy Caching (s)	Adaptive Bitrate Streaming (s)	P2P+CDN Caching (s)
500	14	13	12	10
400	12	11	10	8
300	10	9	8	6
200	8	7	6	4
100	6	5	4	2

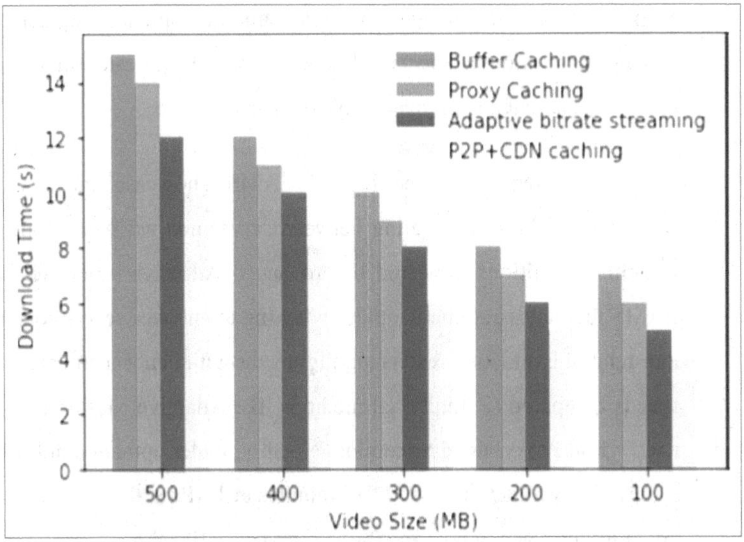

Fig. 3.5 Comparison of download time by various caching techniques for different video sizes

By utilizing the Automatic Mode Selection algorithm in conjunction with the EAMS algorithm over a one-day period, the server mode was selected 60%

of the time, while the P2P mode was chosen 40% of the time. Associated to conventional techniques, this method consistently selected the optimal mode for each download. Furthermore, the proposed technique achieved a 100% successful download completion rate for videos of various sizes.

3.6 Conclusion

This chapter presents an in-depth exploration of the cloud OS-based Enhanced Automated Mode Selection algorithm, detailing its architectural framework, implementation methodologies, and empirical evaluations. The system architecture of EAMS is delineated, emphasizing its seamless integration within the Eye OS cloud environment. This platform enables efficient remote access and task management, crucial for optimizing operations such as video downloads. Videos undergo upload, segmentation, and management through specialized caches, thereby streamlining file retrieval processes and enhancing overall system performance.

Implementation specifics of EAMS showcase its dynamic mode selection capabilities, toggling between server and assistant modes based on real-time conditions. Powered by Advanced Adaptive Mode Selection rules, EAMS facilitates automatic mode switching to enhance server adaptability and throughput. Evaluation results highlight substantial enhancements in download speeds compared to traditional methods like Adaptive Mesh-based Streaming and Hybrid Proxy-aided Streaming. Notably, under optimal conditions, EAMS achieved download times of 02:15 minutes at 1 Mbps, 01:00 minute at 2 Mbps, 00:24 minutes at 5 Mbps, and 00:12 minutes at 10 Mbps.

Furthermore, integrating the Automatic Mode Selection algorithm with EAMS over a one-day period demonstrated adaptive behavior, selecting server mode 60% of the time and P2P mode 40% of the time. This adaptive approach consistently identified the optimal mode for each download; resulting in a remarkable 100% success rate in completing video downloads across diverse file sizes. These findings underscore EAMS as a robust solution for real-time video content delivery, validating its efficiency across varied network conditions and data speeds. Key findings emphasize the synergistic benefits of peer-to-peer and content distribution network caching, enhancing scalability and reducing latency in video delivery. The integrated Automatic Mode Selection algorithm further ensures precise mode selection tailored to each download scenario, reaffirming EAMS as a useful and effective solution for adaptive video streaming in cloud environments.

CHAPTER 4

Optimized Cloud Download Service

4.1 Introduction

This chapter focuses on using advanced caching, data distribution, and bandwidth management techniques to optimize cloud download services within peer-to-peer systems. The objectives of these actions are to enhance system performance overall, reduce latency, and improve content delivery.

4.2 Optimization of Peer-To-Peer System Downloading

4.2.1 Advanced Caching Mechanism

First, it is made sure that the right template is chosen for the job. In order to improve AMS-based cloud downloading services and optimize download times in peer-to-peer systems, a novel intelligent caching mechanism has been developed. This mechanism uses a sophisticated caching strategy based on temporal locality patterns and popularity metrics for video content. The system provides a significant reduction in latency during content retrieval by identifying and caching video content that is in high demand close to end users. The caching mechanism ensures immediate availability by dynamically updating its cache based on real-time fluctuations in content reputation.

The mathematical formula for the caching strategy is symbolized below:

$$\text{Maximize:} \sum_i p_i * X_i \qquad (4.1)$$

$$\text{Subject to:} \sum_i size(v_i) * X_{i \leq} C \qquad (4.2)$$

$$X_i \in \{0, 1\}, \forall i \ (1) \qquad (4.3)$$

In this formula, size (vi) indicates the video's storage size, C indicates the cache capacity, pi indicates the popularity score of video vi, and xi is a binary variable that indicates whether or not video vii is cached (xi=1) or not (xi=0). The objective function prioritizes more popular videos for caching by increasing the sum of the popularity scores of the cached videos. The constraint verifies that the aggregate storage size of the videos that have been cached shouldn't go over the cache's capacity.

The caching strategy solves this optimization problem by determining which videos are the most popular and fit into the available cache size. By moving these videos closer to users, this method meritoriously caches content and lowers network latency during content retrieval., Consequently, by reducing network congestion and bandwidth consumption, the intelligent caching mechanism improves user experience, speeds up download times, lowers latency, and boosts system performance.

Algorithm: Intelligent Catching Strategy

Enter: a list of the videos V={v1, v2,..., vn), Each video's popularity scores: P is equal to {p1, p2,..., pn}. Capacity of cache: C
Output: List of stored videos
Step 1: Arrange videos according to their popularity scores, descending: V' = Sort (V,P)
Step 2: Adjust a cache that is empty: Cache = []
Step 3: Determine the cache's current capacity. Capacity Remaining = C
Step 4: In V', for every video v:
a. If C> size (v):
i. Improve video v to store in the cache: Cache. append(v)
ii. Refresh the available capacity: C is equal to C - size(v).
Step 5: Provide the cached video list back: come back Hold on

4.2.2 Intelligent Data Distribution Algorithm

The goal of the Intelligent Data Distribution algorithm is to maximize the availability of video content in peer-to-peer networks by emphasizing the effective use of network resources. Using machine learning techniques, the algorithm aggressively modifies its data dispersal strategy in real time, taking into account user preferences, popular content, and network conditions. It precisely predicts the demand for video content by using models and historical data, enabling efficient network resource allocation.

This algorithm prioritizes the distribution of popular videos, which speeds up downloads. In order to assess content demand and allocate network resources effectively, it accomplishes this by examining user behavior, content popularity, and network circumstances. Peers with high bandwidth and stability are selected for data distribution based on peer connectivity and available bandwidth. This astute peer selection minimizes obstructions and maximizes download speeds. Consequently, the algorithm effectively increases the P2P system's capability and efficiency.

This study presents a novel data distribution algorithm based on decision trees and the flow diagram is given in **Fig. 4.1**. The process begins with data collection, where relevant data is gathered from various sources. Once the data is collected, the next step is feature extraction, where key attributes or features are identified and extracted from the raw data, which are essential for model building. After extracting the features, the process moves to training data preparation, where the data is preprocessed and organized in a format suitable for model training.

With the training data ready, the model training phase begins. In this phase, a machine learning model is trained using the prepared data, allowing it to learn patterns and relationships within the data. Once training is complete, the model undergoes model evaluation, where its performance is assessed using various metrics to determine its effectiveness.

Following the evaluation, data distribution decision-making takes place. This step involves deciding how the model's predictions or insights will be distributed or used within the system or to end-users. The final step is continuous learning and adaptation, where the model is continually updated and adapted based on new data or changing conditions to maintain its relevance and accuracy. This cycle repeats, ensuring the system remains effective over time, and the process eventually concludes.

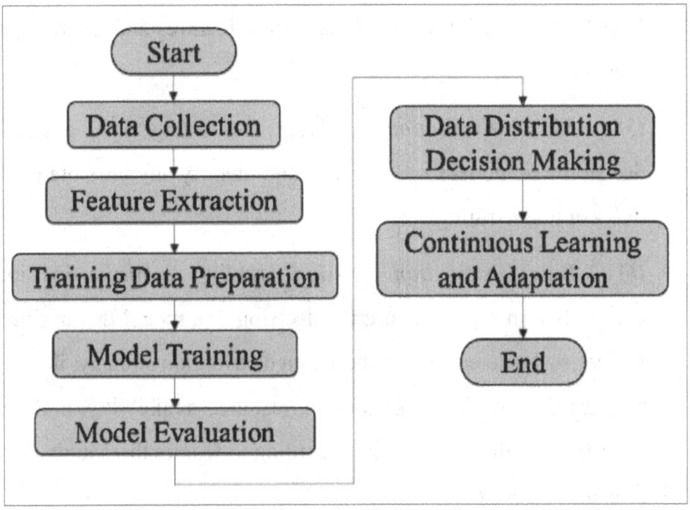

Fig. 4.1 Flow diagram of the Decision Tree-based Data Distribution algorithm

The detailed steps of the algorithm are as follows:

(1) ***Data Collection****:* Compile important information about the network, resources, and workload, including historical workload patterns, bandwidth usage, and network traffic.

(2) ***Feature extraction***: Take relevant structures out of the data that has been gathered, such as throughput, network latency, resource usage, and other factors that affect how data is distributed.

(3) Preparing Training Data: Divide the gathered information into datasets for testing and training. The decision tree model is trained using the training data, and its performance is evaluated using the testing data.

(4) Model Training: Utilizing the training data, train a decision tree model. This entails the decision tree recursively partitioning the data according to features in order to minimize impurity or maximize information gain, and learning the relationships between input features and desired data distribution outcomes.

(5) Model Evaluation: Utilizing the testing data, evaluate the trained decision tree model's performance and identify any possible problems, such as over- or under-fitting.

(6) Data Distribution Decision Making: To make decisions about data distribution in real time, use the decision tree model that has been trained and validated. To determine the best data distribution strategy, the model takes into account the workload distribution, resource availability, and current network conditions. It divides the data according to feature thresholds and allots it to the relevant nodes or resources.

(7) Continuous Learning and Adaptation: To adjust to evolving data distribution patterns and network conditions, periodically retrain the decision tree model using reorganized data. This guarantees that the model's decision-making process is always incorporating the most recent data.

4.2.3 Mathematical Formulation

With dimensionality d, the input features are represented as X=[x1,x2,...,xn], and Y is the corresponding target variable that shows the result of the data distribution. Finding a function f(X)→Y that maps the input features to the target variable is the goal of the decision tree algorithm.

A set of decision rules, each of which is associated with a node in the decision tree, is what makes up a decision tree model. A threshold value θ and a feature index i are associated with each node. The following is one way to write the decision rules:

If $x_i \leq \theta$ then

// left child node

// follow a different path based on the value of x_i else

// right child node

// follow a different path based on the value of x_i

By employing an impurity measure or information gain, the decision tree algorithm improves the choice of the feature index I and the threshold value θ at each node.

The impurity measure can be expressed as Impurity (D), where D is the number of data samples at a specific node. Numerous techniques, such as Gini impurity or entropy, can be used to calculate the impurity measure. For example, this is how the Gini impurity is calculated:

$$\text{Gini}(D) = 1 - \Sigma\,(p(c)^2) \qquad (4.4)$$

Where, the probability of class c in the samples at the node is denoted by p(c).

Until a stopping criterion is met, the decision tree algorithm continuously divides the data based on the selected feature index and threshold value. Either the minimum number of samples in a leaf node or the extreme depth of the tree can be used to define this criterion. Real-time data distribution decisions can be made using the trained decision tree model. The model links the feature values at each node in the tree to the corresponding thresholds in order to move from the root to a leaf node for a new data sample x. A choice or the distribution of data to a specific resource or network node is indicated by the leaf node attained.

4.3 Bandwidth Resource Management

A novel approach to managing bandwidth resources has been developed to optimize and distribute resources for downloading video content in peer-to-peer networks. This method includes a bandwidth management system that fervently allocates available bandwidth according to multiple parameters. The method effectively highlights bandwidth allocation by accounting for variables such as user preferences, video quality, and resource fairness.

In order to ensure a positive viewing experience, the system allots more bandwidth to users with specific preferences or to videos with higher quality requirements. Let B(v) represent the bandwidth needed for video v, P(u) represent user u's preference score, and F(u) represent user u's fairness score. The following can be used to express how bandwidth resources are allocated:

$$Allocate(u, v) = \propto * B(v) + \beta * P(u) + \gamma * F(u) \qquad (4.5)$$

In this case, the weights α, β, and γ control the relative significance of each factor during the allocation process. Better-quality videos are guaranteed to have the resources they need for the best possible viewing experience thanks to the video quality-based allocation technique, which assigns higher bandwidth to videos with higher quality requirements. The importance of video quality is represented by the weight α in the allocation formula.

User preferences are taken into consideration during the allocation process by the user preference-based allocation technique. Advanced bandwidth allocations are provided to users with specific requirements or preferences; the weight β in the allocation formula indicates how important the user's preferences are. The fairness-based allocation technique combines mechanisms to encourage equitable distribution and discourage hoarding of resources. Users are assigned fairness scores based on a number of factors, such as their past use of system resources or contribution. Higher bandwidth allotments are given to users who score higher on fairness. The significance of fairness in the process is represented by the weight γ in the allocation formula.

Algorithm: Bandwidth Resource Management

Enter the following data: available bandwidth, request for video content, video quality requirements (B(v)) for the content, user preferences (P(u)), fairness scores (F(u)), weights (α, β, γ) for video quality, and user preferences.

Output: The requested content's allocated bandwidth

Method:

Step 1: Adjust the weights (α, β, γ) according to user preferences, fairness, and video quality.

Step2: Show the bandwidth that is available.

Get a request for video content in step three.

Step 3: Control the video quality specifications (B(v)) for the content that is being requested.

Step 4: Determine a preference score (P(u)) by analyzing user preferences.

***Step 5*:** Determine fairness scores (F(u)) by considering contributions or user behavior.

Step 6: Use this formula to allocate bandwidth: $(u,v) = \alpha*B(v) + \beta*P(u) + \gamma*F(u)$ allocation

Step 7: Assign the requested content to the designated bandwidth and arrange it accordingly.

Step 8: Examine any restrictions on fairness and adjust the distribution as necessary.

Step 9: Give the user access to the video content.

Step 10: For upcoming requests, review steps 3 through 10.

***Step 11*:** Complete the algorithm for bandwidth resource management.

Through a zealous allocation of available bandwidth based on user preferences, video quality, and fairness, the method improves peer-to-peer system download times for video content. This attests to the effective allocation of resources, which minimizes delays and improves user satisfaction overall.

4.4 Results and Discussion

The advanced caching, intelligent data distribution, and bandwidth resource management methods are thoroughly tested by means of carefully planned experiment. This simulation mimicked a variety of peer-to-peer network conditions to ensure accurate evaluation. The dataset included video content spanning various popularity levels and features, chosen to represent diverse scenarios. Specifically, the dataset comprised five videos, each delineated in **Table 4.1**.

Table 4.1 Trial Dataset

Video	Range	Esteem	Time
1st sample	480p	Low	3 mins
2nd sample	480p	Medium	6 mins
3rd sample	720p	High	8 mins
4th sample	720p	Medium	5 mins
5th sample	1080p	High	10 mins

In order to evaluate the efficacy of the sophisticated caching mechanism, intelligent data distribution algorithm, and bandwidth resource management technique, the experiments replicated the download of video content across the network. **Table 4.2** contains specific information about the network conditions.

By contrasting the time required to retrieve video content from the cache with antiquated caching techniques, the effectiveness of the advanced caching mechanism was assessed. The goal of the bandwidth resource management technique experiments was to assess system performance overall, fairness in resource allocation, and the order of importance for downloading video content.

Table 4.2 System Settings

Metrics	Conditions
Existing Bandwidth	100 Mbps
Bandwidth capacity of each peer	5 Mbps to 20 Mbps
Total number of Peers in the set-up	10 peers
Peer Connectivity	5 peers with steady connectivity and 5 with irregular or unpredictable connectivity

User satisfaction, fairness index, and bandwidth utilization were among the many variables that were meticulously collected. The outcomes were thoroughly examined and contrasted with current methodologies, offering insightful perspectives on the advantages, drawbacks, and effects of the suggested strategies for maximizing download speeds in peer-to-peer networks.

4.4.1 Performance Evaluation

To evaluate efficacy, performance metrics such as cache hit ratio, latency, and average download time were created and examined. Similarly, download speeds, download completion times, data transfer rates, and resource usage were calculated to evaluate the efficacy of the intelligent data distribution algorithm. The baseline methods served as comparative standards. The suggested method is contrasted with other methods that are currently in use, such as Fair Resource Allocation (FRA), Dynamic Caching (DC), Distributed hash tables (DHT), Intelligent data distribution (IDD), Advanced Caching (AC), and Bandwidth resource management (BM). Adaptive Intelligent Video

Distribution technique (AIVD) consistently outperform existing methods in terms of average download time across five different samples.

4.4.1.1 Average Download Time

The average download times for each technique are compared, comparing the suggested methods with individual and baseline approaches, as shown in **Table 4.3**. It gives the five distinct samples' average download times. On the other hand, **Fig. 4.2** compares the suggested methods with individual and baseline approaches and shows the average download times in seconds for each technique. It gives the five distinct samples' average download times. In terms of average download time, the suggested method performs better than Advanced Caching (**Wu et al., 2019**), Intelligent data distribution (**Zhang et al., 2020**), Bandwidth resource management (**Taheri et al., 2016**), Dynamic caching (**Niu et al., 2015**), Distributed hash tables (**Thompson et al., 2023**), and Fair resource allocation (**Rizvi et al., 2014**) techniques in terms of average download time.

Table 4.3 Comparison of Average Download Time for Different Techniques in seconds

Technique	1st sample (s)	2nd sample (s)	3rd sample (s)	4th sample (s)	5th sample (s)
AC	125	100	75	50	70
IDD	150	125	100	75	50
BRM	175	150	125	100	75
DC	160	135	110	85	60
DHT	200	175	150	125	100
FRA	180	155	130	105	80
AIVD	100	75	50	25	30

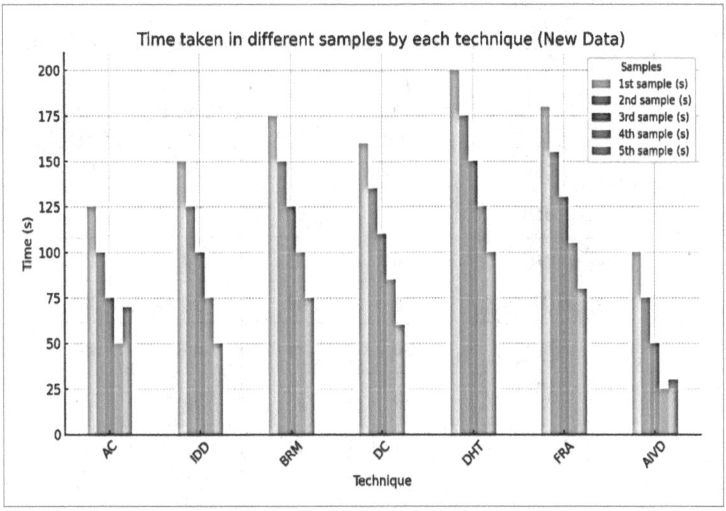

Fig. 4.2 Average download time evaluation

4.4.1.2 Latency

Latency is the time it takes for data to travel from its source to its destination. It's essentially a measure of delay, and lower latency means faster response times. Latency is measured in milliseconds (ms) and can be influenced by various factors, including the distance between the source and destination, the number of devices data must pass through, and network congestion.

The comparison of latency for various techniques, measured in milliseconds, is validated in **Table 4.4** by contrasting the suggested methods with individual and baseline approaches. The reduction in latency that the suggested techniques achieve over the baseline methods is shown in **Fig. 4.3**. It shows each technique's latency in milliseconds, demonstrating how well the suggested approaches work to shorten the time required for content recovery. The suggested method is the most efficient because it has the lowest latency and the most consistent latency. While DC and DHT have the highest and most variable latencies, AC also performs well.

Table 4.4 Comparison of Latency for Different Techniques

Technique	1st sample (ms)	2nd sample (ms)	3rd sample (ms)	4th sample (ms)	5th sample (ms)
AC	30	25	20	15	10
IDD	35	30	25	20	15
BRM	40	35	30	25	20
DC	35	40	35	30	25
DHT	50	45	40	35	30
FRA	40	35	30	25	20
AIVD	25	20	15	10	5

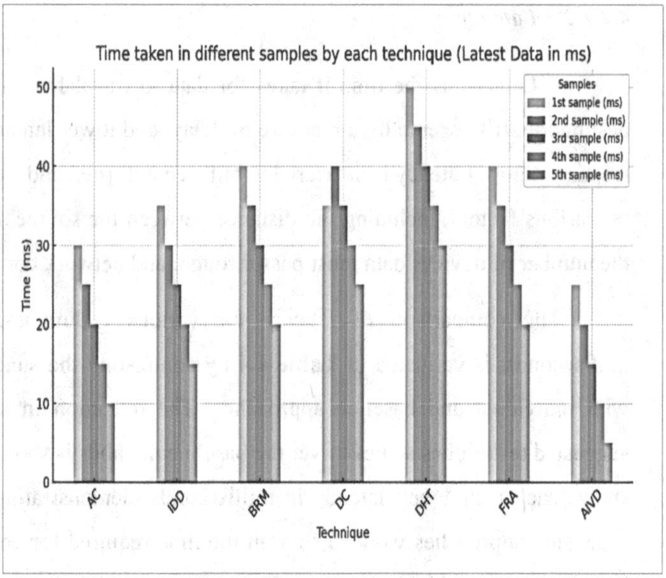

Fig. 4.3 Latency Comparison

4.4.1.3 Cache Hit Ratio

This is an essential metric for assessing how well a system's caching mechanisms are working. The percentage of requested data that is successfully repossessed from the cache as opposed to being fetched from the original source is indicated by the Cache Hit Ratio. A high cache hit ratio indicates that a significant portion of the requested data is found in the cache and is easily accessible. **Table 4.5** presents the percentage Cache Hit Ratio for various techniques, contrasting the suggested approaches with individual and baseline methods. The cache hit ratios of the suggested models and the current models are compared in **Fig. 4.4**. The suggested method is the best at keeping a high cache hit ratio across various samples, indicating its dependability and resilience in caching processes.

Table 4.5 Comparison of Cache Hit Ratio for Different Techniques

Technique	1st sample (p)	2nd sample (p)	3rd sample (p)	4th sample (p)	5th sample (p)
AC	77	82	84	80	82
IDD	83	82	83	79	81
BRM	81	82	83	80	83
DC	77	83	82	78	80
DHT	83	84	83	80	84
FRA	82	83	84	81	83
AIVD	82	85	84	81	84

4.4.1.4 Download Completion Time

It describes the total amount of time needed for a video to finish downloading from its original location to the user's device. This is an important metric because it consistently affects user satisfaction. Shorter download times enhance the overall experience by enabling quicker access to the desired content, while longer download times may cause user obstruction and trouble.

Table 4.6 compares the suggested methods with individual and baseline approaches by displaying the Download Completion Time for various techniques.

The AIVD suggested methods' download completion times are compared to those of the current approaches in **Fig. 4.5**. The download completion times of the suggested method are the fastest and most reliable, surpassing those of AC, IDD, BRM, DC, and DHT.

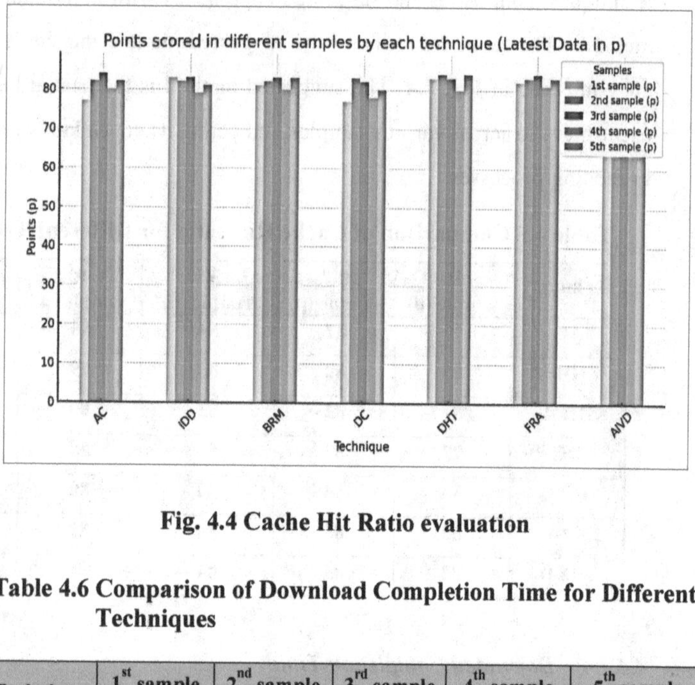

Fig. 4.4 Cache Hit Ratio evaluation

Table 4.6 Comparison of Download Completion Time for Different Techniques

Technique	1st sample (s)	2nd sample (s)	3rd sample (s)	4th sample (s)	5th sample (s)
AC	125	75	50	100	125
IDD	150	100	75	50	125
BRM	175	100	75	50	125
DC	150	100	75	50	125
DHT	150	100	75	50	100
AIVD	100	70	70	45	87

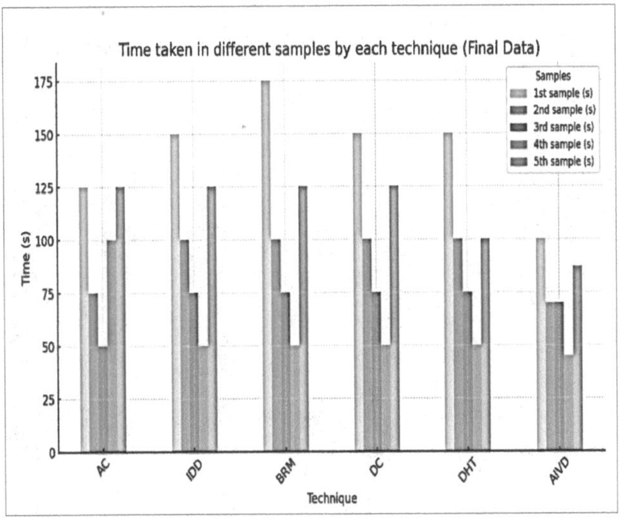

Fig. 4.5 Download Completion Time assessment

The data transfer rates of the suggested methods and those of the current approaches are compared in **Fig. 4.6**. When compared to other techniques, the suggested method achieves the fastest and most reliable download completion times.

Table 4.7 Comparison of Data Transfer Rate for Different Techniques

Technique	1st sample (mbps)	2nd sample (mbps)	3rd sample (mbps)	4th sample (mbps)	5th sample (mbps)
AC	97.54	85.06	69.17	79.61	72.32
IDD	86.6	90.4	75.21	83.32	100.38
BRM	79.93	56.03	86.24	87.8	78.53
DC	57.8	98.5	81.6	90.26	73.25
DHT	57.8	96.62	74.56	74.98	117.44
FRA	52.9	65.62	90.59	90.71	73.28
AIVD	98.73	103.31	92.09	104.97	118.62

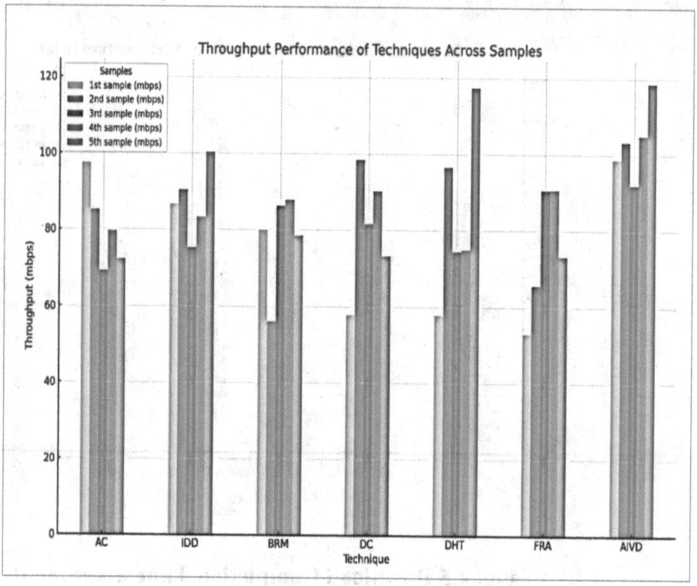

Fig. 4.6 Data Transfer Comparison (in Mbps)

4.4.1.6 Resource Utilization Metrics

The resource utilization metrics, including bandwidth utilization and resource allocation fairness, are displayed for each technique in **Table 4.8**. It shows these metrics side by side for every approach, highlighting how beneficial the suggested bandwidth resource management strategy is for resource allocation optimization. **Table 4.3** makes it clear that the suggested method performs best with the highest bandwidth utilization (92%) and the highest level of fairness. Bandwidth Resource Management exhibits strong performance as well, with high fairness and 89% utilization. On the other hand, Dynamic Caching exhibits the lowest fairness and bandwidth utilization (73%).

These variables have an indirect impact on scalability, cost-effectiveness, bandwidth usage, and system performance.

Table 4.8 Resource Utilization Metrics

Methodology	Resource Allotment Equality	Bandwidth Consumption (%)
Advanced Caching	Medium	74%
Bandwidth resource management	High	89%
Distributed hash tables	Medium	81%
Dynamic caching	Low	73%
Fair resource allocation	Medium	76%
Intelligent data distribution	Medium	82%
Proposed Decision-tree technique	High	92%

In the end, they help peer-to-peer systems achieve optimal resource utilization and improved user experience.

4.5 Conclusion

This chapter introduces an intelligent Decision-Tree based data distribution caching mechanism designed to minimize download latency by strategically caching popular video content closer to end-users. This mechanism dynamically updates its cache on the basis of real-time popularity metrics, confirming rapid content retrieval while adhering to storage constraints. By prioritizing high-demand videos for caching, the system effectively reduces network congestion and enhances overall performance.

Additionally, the chapter explores an innovative data distribution algorithm that optimizes video delivery across P2P networks using decision tree models. This algorithm adapts data distribution strategies based on network conditions and user behaviors, selecting optimal peers for content distribution to maximize download speeds. By leveraging machine learning techniques, it accurately forecasts content demand and allocates resources accordingly, resulting in improved system efficiency and user satisfaction. Furthermore, a unique bandwidth resource management technique is introduced to dynamically allocate bandwidth on the basis of video quality requirements, user preferences, and fairness principles. This approach ensures equitable resource allocation while prioritizing high-quality video downloads, thereby enhancing the streaming experience and optimizing resource utilization. Experimental evaluations validate the effectiveness of these techniques in reducing average download times, improving cache hit ratios, and enhancing overall system performance across varied network conditions.

CHAPTER 5

Integrating Machine Learning in Peer-to-Peer Video Content Systems for Predictive Caching and Dynamic Data Distribution

The ever-growing demand for high-quality video content places significant strain on peer-to-peer video content distribution systems. Traditional approaches struggle to handle the increasing volume and diverse content types, resulting in bottlenecks and degraded user experience. This chapter suggests a novel approach that leverages machine learning for predictive caching and dynamic data distribution within P2P video content systems. In this research introduce the Dynamic Adaptive Caching and Distribution Engine, a hybrid algorithm that integrates three key ML modules: Content Popularity Prediction Module (CPPM), User Demand Forecasting Module, and Resource Optimization Module (UDFM). CPPM utilizes time series forecasting techniques to predict content popularity, allowing for preemptive caching of popular videos closer to potential requesters. UDFM employs gradient boosting machines to forecast user demand in different network zones, ensuring content is distributed efficiently to meet anticipated requests. ROM leverages deep Q-networks for real-time optimization of network resources and data distribution paths. A detailed explanation of the D-ACADE algorithm is provided, including its operation workflow, key components, and the underlying mathematical formulations. This chapter concludes by discussing the potential benefits of D-ACADE, including its adaptability, scalability, and efficiency in enhancing P2P video content delivery.

5.1 Introduction

The popularity of online video streaming has surged in recent years, driven by the propagation of high-speed internet access and growing availability of high-quality content. A peer-to-peer video content distribution system plays a crucial part in facilitating the demand by leveraging the collective resources of participating users. However, traditional P2P systems face challenges in keeping pace with the ever-increasing volume and diverse content types. These challenges often manifest as bottlenecks, long download times, and buffering delays, ultimately degrading user experience.

This chapter presents a novel approach for enhancing P2P video content delivery through machine learning-driven caching and dynamic data distribution. We propose the Dynamic Adaptive Caching and Distribution Engine (D-ACADE), a hybrid algorithm that integrates machine learning to anticipate user requests and content popularity. D-ACADE proactively caches popular content closer to potential requesters, while dynamically optimizing data distribution paths on the basis of the real-time network conditions and user behavior. This proactive approach minimizes download times and buffering delays, leading to a further seamless and efficient video streaming experience for users.

5.2 Background and Motivation

The success of P2P video content distribution systems hinges on their ability to efficiently locate and deliver requested content. Traditional approaches rely on reactive mechanisms where content is searched for upon user request. This reactive approach leads to significant delays, especially for popular content or in congested network environments.

To address these limitations, researchers have explored proactive caching techniques, where frequently accessed content is preemptively stored closer to potential requesters. However, traditional caching strategies often rely on static rules or historical averages, which is ineffective in capturing the self-motivated nature of user demand and content popularity.

Machine learning offers a promising approach for overcoming these limitations. ML algorithms analyze large datasets of historical user behavior and content access patterns to identify trends and predict future demand. This predictive capability allows for more informed caching decisions, enabling content to be preemptively stored in strategic locations to minimize retrieval times.This chapter leverages the power of machine learning to develop a novel approach for P2P video content delivery. We propose the D-ACADE algorithm, which integrates three key ML modules to achieve both predictive caching and dynamic data distribution.

5.3 The Dynamic Adaptive Caching and Distribution Engine (D-ACADE)

D-ACADE is a hybrid algorithm designed to optimize caching and data distribution within P2P video content systems. It leverages machine learning to predict content popularity, forecast user demand, and dynamically allocate network resources in real-time. **Fig. 5.1** presents the proposed model architecture.

The process begins with the Start phase, where the system is initialized and prepared for the subsequent tasks. Following this, the first crucial step involves Pre-process data feature engineering. Here, raw data is carefully processed and transformed through feature engineering. This step is vital as it involves selecting and creating relevant features that enhance the predictive accuracy of the machine learning models, which will be used later in the workflow.

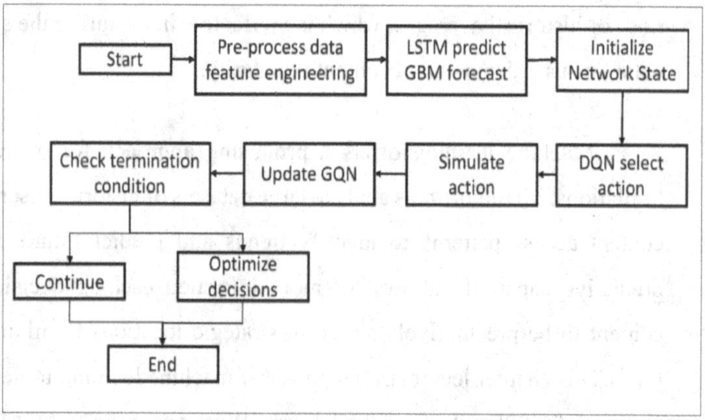

Fig. 5.1 D-ACADE model architecture

Next, the LSTM predict GBM forecast phase utilizes an LSTM model to make predictions based on the pre-processed data. The LSTM model, known for its capability to capture temporal dependencies, forecasts future trends or states of the system, potentially using methods like GBM for time-series predictions. Once these predictions are made, the Initialize Network State step sets up the initial conditions of the network, incorporating the predicted outcomes. This state initialization includes all relevant parameters that define the network's operational environment, which are critical for the upcoming simulations.

The process then moves to the Simulate action phase, where the system simulates various factions within the initialized network state. These simulations provide insights into how different actions might affect the network, allowing for a risk-free exploration of potential outcomes. After simulations, the DQN select action step comes into play. Here, a DQN model selects the optimal action based on the simulated scenarios. DQN, a reinforcement learning algorithm, uses past experiences to inform decision-making, aiming to maximize long-term rewards. Following this, the Update GQN step updates the Generative Query Network with new information gathered from the simulation and the selected actions, ensuring that the network model remains accurate and up-to-date.

The system then checks the termination condition to determine whether the optimization process should continue or conclude. If the conditions for termination are met—such as reaching a specific goal or completing a set number of iterations—the process will end. However, if these conditions are not satisfied, the system proceeds to the Optimize decisions phase, where it refines and optimizes its decisions based on the latest network state and simulations. This iterative process continues, looping back to earlier steps as needed, until the optimal solution is found or the termination criteria are fulfilled, ultimately leading to the End of the workflow.

D-ACADE comprises three core modules:

5.3.1 Content Popularity Prediction Module (CPPM)

CPPM analyzes historical access patterns of video content within the P2P network. This data might include factors such as the frequency of access to specific content, time of day variations in demand, and user demographics. By analyzing these historical trends, CPPM utilizes LSTM networks to estimate the future popularity of various content items. Predicting content popularity allows D-ACADE to cache popular videos closer to potential requesters proactively. This preemptive caching strategy significantly reduces download times and buffering delays, particularly for content experiencing a surge in demand.

5.3.2 User Demand Forecasting Module (UDFM)

UDFM is a module that analyzes user behavior and interaction data to predict the demand for video content in different network zones. This module takes into account factors such as user location, historical access patterns within specific regions, and the type of content typically accessed by users in those zones. To make these predictions, UDFM uses machine learning algorithms, comprising Gradient Boosting Machines (GBMs).The benefits of UDFM are significant. By forecasting user demand, D-ACADE can optimize data distribution by prioritizing content delivery paths that cater to anticipated user requests. This proactive approach ensures that content is readily available in network zones where demand is expected to be high, minimizing delays and optimizing resource utilization.

5.3.3 Resource Optimization Module (ROM)

ROM plays a critical role in dynamically allocating network resources and optimizing data distribution paths in real-time. This module unceasingly displays network conditions, including factors like bandwidth availability, congestion levels, and node capacities. Leveraging Deep Q-Networks (DQN), a type of deep reinforcement learning, ROM makes real-time decisions on resource allocation and data routing. The real-time decision-making capabilities of ROM enable D-ACADE to adapt to dynamic network conditions and user behavior. By continuously analyzing network data and user requests, ROM ensures efficient resource utilization and optimizes data distribution paths to minimize latency and maximize user satisfaction.

5.4 D-ACADE Operation Workflow

D-ACADE operates through a continuous feedback loop that ensures ongoing optimization of caching and data distribution strategies.

Here's a breakdown of the key steps involved:

5.4.1 Data Collection

D-ACADE continuously gathers data on various aspects of the P2P network, including historical user access patterns, content access logs, and real-time network conditions (bandwidth, latency).

5.4.2 Pre-processing and Feature Engineering

The collected data undergoes cleaning and feature engineering to extract relevant characteristics that influence content popularity, user demand, and network optimization. Features might include user demographics, historical access frequency for specific content, temporal patterns of access, and network node capacities.

5.4.3 Prediction and Forecasting

CPPM utilizes the pre-processed data to train the LSTM network, enabling it to forecast future popularity scores for various video content. UDFM leverages GBMs to analyze user behavior data and forecast demand levels for content in different network zones.

5.4.4 Dynamic Optimization

ROM utilizes real-time network data and the predictions from CPPM and UDFM to make real-time decisions on caching and data distribution. Through a DQN-based reward system, ROM optimizes resource allocation to minimize data transfer costs and maximize user satisfaction (e.g., minimizing buffering and download times).

5.4.5 Feedback Loop

The performance of the caching and distribution approaches is continuously evaluated. Insights from this feedback are utilized to retrain and refine the ML models (CPPM, UDFM) within D-ACADE. This feedback loop ensures that the system adapts to evolving user behavior, content popularity trends, and network conditions.

5.5 D-ACADE: A Detailed Look at The Algorithm

A detailed explanation of the D-ACADE algorithm is provided here, along with information regarding comprehensive implementation. This section delves into the Pseudocode representation and mathematical formulations underpinning the algorithm's core functionalities.

5.5.1 Pseudocode

The following presents a high-level Pseudocode outlining the core functionalities of D-ACADE:

Algorithm D-ACADE(Data, NetworkParams)

Inputs:
Data: Historical user access data, content access patterns
NetworkParams: Current network conditions and system configuration parameters
Outputs:
CachingDecisions: Optimized caching locations for video content
DataPaths: Optimized data distribution paths
Begin
Step 1*: Data Preparation*
PreparedData<- Preprocess(Data)
Features <- FeatureEngineering(PreparedData)
Step 2: *Predict Content Popularity*
PopularityScores<- LSTM_Predict(Features)
Step 3: *Forecast User Demand*
DemandForecast<- GBM_Forecast(Features)
Step 4*: Optimize Resource Allocation using DQN*
NetworkState<- InitializeNetworkState(NetworkParams)
For each epoch:
Action <- DQN_SelectAction(NetworkState, Policy)
NewNetworkState, Reward <- SimulateAction(NetworkState, Action)
UpdateDQN(NetworkState, Action, Reward, NewNetworkState)
NetworkState<- NewNetworkState
Step 5*: Output Decisions*
CachingDecisions<-DetermineCachingLocations(PopularityScores, DemandForecast)

DataPaths<- OptimizeDataDistributionPaths(DemandForecast, NetworkState)
Return CachingDecisions, DataPaths
End

- **Steps 1 and 2:** These steps focus on data preparation and content popularity prediction. The raw data undergoes pre-processing and feature engineering to extract relevant features. The LSTM network within CPPM then utilizes the preprocessed data to predict future popularity scores for various video content items.

- **Step 3:** User demand forecasting is addressed in this step. The GBM model in UDFM analyzes the preprocessed data to forecast user demand levels for content within different network zones.

- **Step 4:** This step deals with real-time resource optimization using DQN within ROM. First, the network state is initialized based on current network parameters. Then, an iterative process occurs where DQN selects an action (e.g., allocate bandwidth, adjust caching locations) on the basis of the current network state and a defined policy. The action is simulated, resulting in an innovative network state and a reward signal which reflects the effectiveness of the action. The DQN model is then updated based on the experience gained (action, reward, new state). This iterative process allows ROM to learn and optimize resource allocation strategies continuously.
- **Step 5:** Finally, D-ACADE leverages the predictions from CPPM and UDFM along with the optimized network state from ROM to determine optimal caching locations and data distribution paths. These decisions are then returned as the algorithm's output.

5.5.2 *Mathematical Formulations*

Here, we delve into the mathematical formulations that underpin specific functionalities within D-ACADE:

5.5.2.1 *Content Popularity Prediction (LSTM):*

The LSTM network within CPPM is typically trained to minimize a loss function commonly used in regression problems. This loss function can be represented as:

$$L(\theta) = \frac{1}{N}\sum_{i=1}^{N}(y_i - \hat{y}_i)^2 \tag{5.1}$$

Where:

- θ represents the parameters of the LSTM model.
- N represents the number of training samples.
- y_i represents the actual popularity score for content item i.
- $\hat{y}_i$ represents the predicted popularity score for content item i.

5.5.2.1.1 *Reinforcement Learning (DQN):*

The Deep Q-Network (DQN) employed in ROM utilizes the Bellman equation to optimize the below mentioned loss function:

$$L(\theta) = E\left[\left(r + \gamma \max_{a'} Q(s', a'; \theta^-) - Q(s, a; \theta)\right)^2\right] \tag{5.2}$$

Where:

- r represents the immediate reward received after taking action a in state s.
- γ represents the discount factor ($0 < \gamma \leq 1$).

- $Q(s, a; \theta)$ represents the current estimate of the Q-value for taking action a in state s with parameters θ.
- $Q(s', a'; \theta^{-})$ represents the Q-value of the next state s' as estimated by a target network with parameters θ^{-}.

This loss function guides DQN to learn and select actions that maximize the long-term reward within the dynamic network environment.

The first equation measures the dissimilarity between the actual and expected popularity scores, guiding the LSTM network in CPPM to learn and improve its prediction accuracy. The second equation represents the core principle behind DQN in ROM. It aims to minimize the difference between the expected future reward (considering the discount factor γ) and the current estimate of the Q-value. Through this process, DQN learns to make optimal resource allocation decisions that maximize long-term system performance within the P2P network. By combining these Pseudocode steps and mathematical formulations, D-ACADE establishes a comprehensive framework for optimizing caching and data distribution in P2P video content delivery systems.

5.6 Results and Discussion

Table 5.1 displays the popularity scores over time, illustrating the changes in popularity from January 1st to January 4th. **Fig. 5.2** is a graphical representation of the popularity of video content items over different dates. It demonstrates trends and variations in user engagement. Each data point on the plot corresponds to a specific date, providing a clear timeline view of popularity trends over time. The y-axis labels display time values in a short HH:MM format, showing the associated time of day for each popularity score. This reveals patterns of content consumption throughout the day. The use of markers ('o') and properly formatted axis labels enhance the clarity and readability of the plot, making it easier to interpret the data. By combining date-based popularity scores with time-specific engagement metrics, the visualization offers valuable insights into user behavior patterns and preferences across different time periods.

Table 5.1 Popularity Scores over Time

Date	Popularity Score
January 1st 00:00	0.50
January 2nd 00:00	0.70
January 2nd 12:00	0.75
January 3rd 00:00	0.80
January 3rd 12:00	0.60
January 4th 00:00	0.50

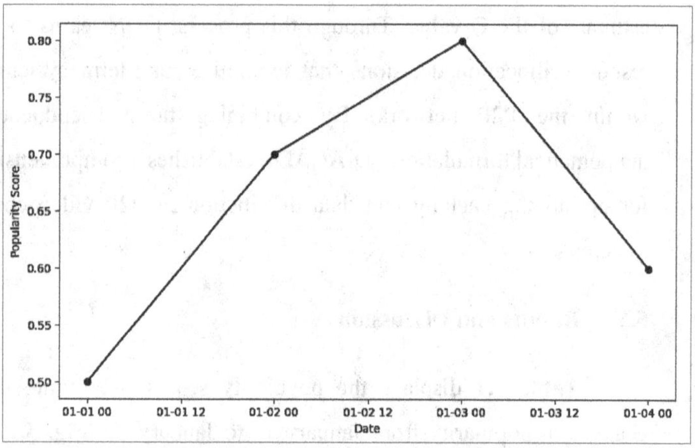

Fig. 5.2 Popularity of video content over time

Table 5.2 exhibits the comparison of the expected demand levels across various regions. The bar plot in **Fig. 5.3** is an effective tool for comparing the expected demand levels across various regions, presenting a clear visual representation of the differing demand projections. Regions with higher bar heights indicate the areas where high demand is expected. This information helps prioritize resource allocation and content distribution strategies in accordance with anticipated demand. The visualization also highlights geographic preferences or trends in user demand, enabling tailored content delivery strategies based on regional preferences. By visualizing demand forecasts, stakeholders can make well-versed decisions about resource allocation, content caching, and network optimization to meet the expected demand levels. The plot facilitates strategic planning by offering insights into regional demand dynamics, supporting effective resource management and operational decisions.

Table 5.2 Comparison of the Expected Demand Levels Across Various Regions

Region	Demand Forecast
Region A	100
Region B	80
Region C	120
Region D	90

For example, in the table below illustrates how holidays can affect demand in different states, leading to either an increase or decrease in the forecasted demand. Each state has different holidays that impact their demand differently

Table 5.3 provides the Resource allocation over Epochs. Whereas, **Fig. 5.4** visually illustrates how bandwidth allocation and cache utilization change over time in 10 distinct epochs.

By displaying these two metrics on the same graph, the plot makes it easy to compare them across different epochs. Each data point on the plot represents a specific epoch, allowing for the identification of patterns and fluctuations in resource allocation at each time step. The y-axis is designed to display specific intervals, which makes it easier to interpret the resource allocation values within the plotted range. With its concise presentation and limited number of epochs, this plot provides a clear visualization of resource allocation dynamics, enabling a better understanding of temporal trends in bandwidth and cache usage.

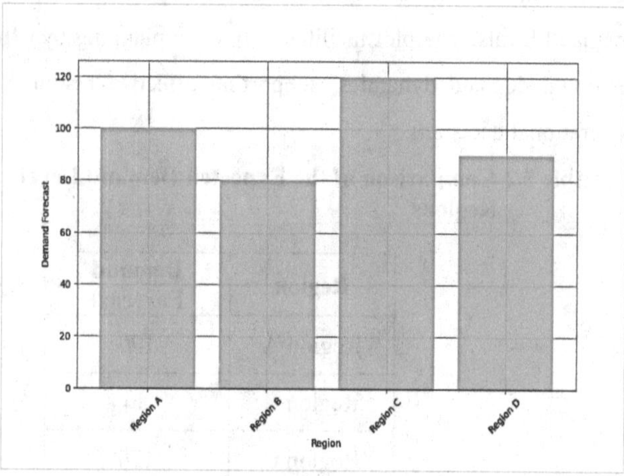

Fig. 5.3 Forecast demand vs. various regions

Table 5.3 Resource Allocation over Epochs

Epoch	Bandwidth Allocation	Cache Utilization
1	0.5	0.4
2	0.7	0.5
3	0.8	0.6
4	0.7	0.7
5	0.9	0.3
6	0.8	0.2
7	0.6	0.4
8	0.6	0.5
9	0.8	0.5
10	0.7	0.6

For example

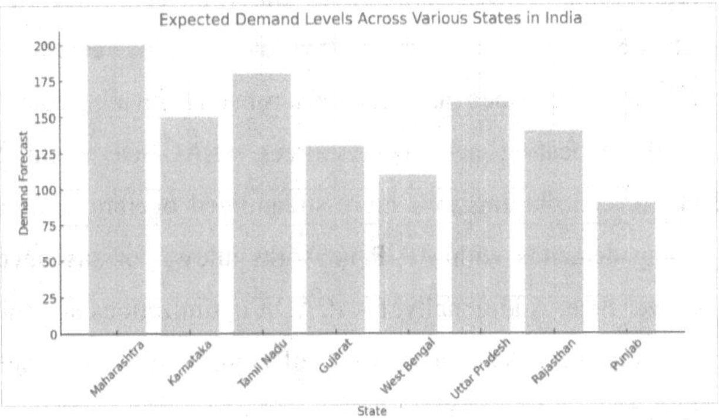

Fig. 5.4 Forecast demand vs. various regions in India

The graph **(Fig. 5.4)** is a bar chart titled "Expected Demand Levels Across Various States in India." It illustrates the demand forecast for different states in India. his graph provides valuable insights into how different states in India are expected to require resources or services, helping in planning and resource allocation.

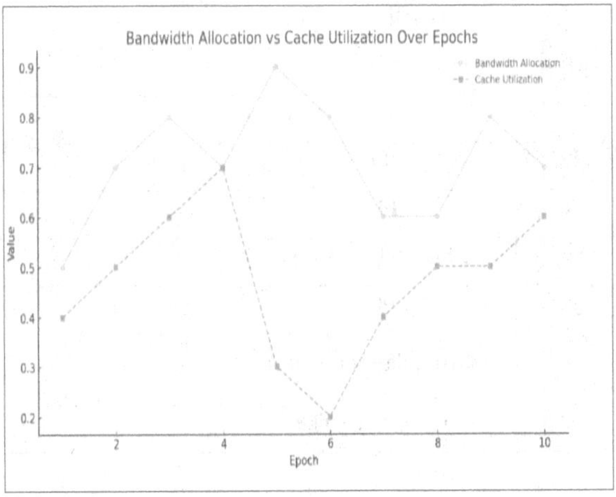

Fig. 5.5 Bandwidth allocation and cache utilization

D-ACADE optimization of data distribution leads to a reduction in network traffic, thereby enhancing overall efficiency, as exposed in **Fig. 5.6**. The relationship of Network Load and Buffering Time over the Year is shown in **Table 5.4**. This improvement translates into decreased buffering times, ensuring smoother video playback and ultimately elevating user satisfaction. By efficiently allocating network resources, D-ACADE optimizes bandwidth utilization, contributing to a more streamlined operation. Its adaptability to increasing demands within P2P networks allows for sustained performance levels over time. Additionally, D-ACADE optimizations not only reduce costs but also enhance user engagement, offering significant benefits to content providers.

Table 5.4 Network Load and Buffering Time over the Year

Month	Network Load (Mbps)	Buffering Time without D-ACADE (seconds)	Buffering Time with D-ACADE (seconds)
Jan	150	6	3
Feb	180 (increased demand)	8	4.5
Mar	140	5	2.8
Apr	160 (holiday spike)	7	3.8
May	120	4	2.5
Jun	170 (special event)	8	4.2
Jul	100	3	1.8
Aug	130	5	2.6
Sep	200 (peak season)	9	5
Oct	90	3	1.7
Nov	160 (holiday shopping)	7	3.8
Dec	180 (holiday spike)	8	4.3

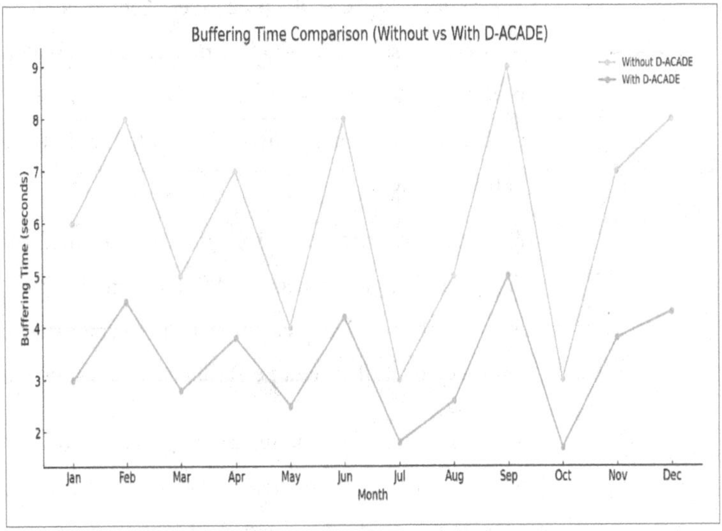

Fig. 5.6 D-ACADE data distribution

5.7 Benefits of D-ACADE

D-ACADE offers several advantages over traditional P2P content delivery approaches:

- ***Adaptability:*** D-ACADE leverages machine learning to dynamically adapt to changing user behavior and content popularity trends. This real-time adaptation ensures that caching and distribution strategies remain optimized even in the face of evolving network conditions.

- ***Scalability:*** The design of D-ACADE makes it inherently scalable to handle large P2P networks with a growing user base and increasing content volume. The machine learning models within D-ACADE can be continuously trained on new data, allowing them to maintain their effectiveness as the network scales.

- ***Efficiency:*** D-ACADE proactive caching and dynamic data distribution strategies significantly reduce download times and buffering delays for users. This efficiency translates to improved user experience and satisfaction with the P2P video content delivery system.

- ***Reduced Network Load*:** By optimizing content placement and data distribution paths, D-ACADE minimizes unnecessary network traffic. This reduction in network load contributes to improved overall system performance and resource utilization.

- ***Cost-Effectiveness:*** The improved efficiency of D-ACADE lead to cost savings for content providers by reducing bandwidth consumption and server load. Additionally, the reduced buffering times improve user engagement and potentially lead to increased advertising revenue.

5.8 Conclusion

This chapter presented D-ACADE, a novel approach for enhancing P2P video content delivery through machine learning-driven caching and dynamic data distribution. D-ACADE integrates three key machine learning modules, CPPM, UDFM, and ROM, to achieve proactive content caching, user demand forecasting, and real-time resource optimization. By leveraging machine learning, D-ACADE offers significant advantages over traditional P2P content delivery systems, including adaptability, scalability, efficiency, reduced network load, and cost-effectiveness.

CHAPTER 6

Summary & Conclusion and Scope for Further Study

This chapter serves to be the conclusion of the work that highlights the key findings and future scope or direction of the proposed research work.

6.1 Summary & Conclusion

The rapid evolution of video content downloading, particularly through P2P and cloud-based systems, has revolutionized the way users access and consume digital media. By leveraging the combined strengths of cloud infrastructure and peer-to-peer networks, these systems have dramatically enhanced scalability, efficiency, and user satisfaction.

Primarily, an in-depth exploration of the cloud OS-based Enhanced Automated Mode Selection algorithm, detailing its architectural framework, implementation methodologies, and empirical evaluations is made. The system architecture of EAMS is delineated, emphasizing its seamless integration within the Eye OS cloud environment. This platform enables efficient remote access and task management, crucial for optimizing operations such as video downloads. Videos undergo upload, segmentation, and management through specialized caches, thereby streamlining file retrieval processes and enhancing overall system performance.

Implementation specifics of EAMS showcase its dynamic mode selection capabilities, toggling between server and assistant modes based on real-time conditions. Powered by Advanced Adaptive Mode Selection rules, EAMS facilitates automatic mode switching to enhance server adaptability and throughput. Evaluation results highlight substantial enhancements in download speeds compared to traditional methods like Adaptive Mesh-based Streaming and Hybrid Proxy-aided Streaming. Notably, under optimal conditions, EAMS achieved download times of 02:15 minutes at 1 Mbps, 01:00 minute at 2 Mbps, 00:24 minutes at 5 Mbps, and 00:12 minutes at 10 Mbps.

Furthermore, integrating the Automatic Mode Selection algorithm with EAMS over a one-day period demonstrated adaptive behavior, selecting server mode 60% of the time and P2P mode 40% of the time. This adaptive approach consistently identified the optimal mode for each download; resulting in a remarkable 100% success rate in completing video downloads across diverse file sizes. These findings underscore EAMS as a robust solution for real-time video content delivery, validating its efficiency across varied network conditions and data speeds. Key findings emphasize the synergistic benefits of peer-to-peer and content distribution network caching, enhancing scalability and reducing latency in video delivery. The integrated Automatic Mode Selection algorithm further ensures precise mode selection tailored to each download scenario, reaffirming EAMS as an adaptable and effective resolution for adaptive video streaming in cloud environments.

As the second work, an intelligent Decision-Tree based data distribution caching mechanism is designed to minimize download latency by strategically caching popular video content closer to end-users. This mechanism vigorously updates its cache on the basis of real-time attractiveness metrics, guaranteeing rapid content retrieval while adhering to storage constraints. By prioritizing high-demand videos for caching, the system effectively reduces network congestion and enhances overall performance. An innovative data distribution algorithm that optimizes video delivery across P2P networks using decision tree models was also elaborated additionally. This algorithm adapts data distribution strategies based on network conditions and user behaviors, selecting optimal peers for content distribution to maximize download speeds. By leveraging machine learning techniques, it accurately forecasts content demand and allocates resources accordingly, resulting in improved system efficiency and user satisfaction.

Furthermore, a unique bandwidth resource management technique was introduced to dynamically allocate bandwidth on the basis of video quality requirements, user inclinations, and fairness principles. This approach ensures equitable resource allocation while prioritizing high-quality video downloads, thereby enhancing the streaming experience and optimizing resource utilization. Experimental evaluations validate the effectiveness of these techniques in reducing average download times, improving cache hit ratios, and enhancing overall system performance across varied network conditions.

Finally, Dynamic Adaptive Caching and Distribution Engine, another innovative approach, integrating three key ML modules: the Content Popularity Prediction Module, the User Demand Forecasting Module, and the Resource Optimization Module is proposed. CPPM employs time series forecasting to predict content popularity, allowing preemptive caching of popular videos closer to potential requesters. UDFM utilizes gradient boosting machines to forecast user demand across different network zones, ensuring efficient content distribution. ROM leverages deep Q-networks for real-time optimization of network resources and data distribution paths. These methodologies collectively enhance P2P cloud-based video content downloading, optimizing caching and distribution strategies, and significantly reducing download times and buffering delays. D-ACADE optimizations lead to reduced network traffic, smoother video playback, effective bandwidth utilization, and adaptation to increasing demands within P2P networks, maintaining performance. Additionally, D-ACADE proactive caching and optimized distribution significantly reduce download times and buffering delays, enhancing user satisfaction and overall system performance. By minimizing network load and reducing bandwidth consumption, D-ACADE results in cost savings for content providers, improving resource utilization and potentially increasing revenue through enhanced user engagement.

6.2 Scope for Further Study

Future work in video content downloading systems and predictive modeling presents exciting opportunities for further advancements. Enhancing the scalability and adaptability of these systems to accommodate varying network conditions and user demands is critical., Developing sophisticated algorithms that dynamically adjust caching and distribution strategies in real-time can significantly improve performance. By leveraging advanced machine learning techniques, future systems could predict network congestion and user demand patterns, optimizing resource allocation. Moreover, scalable architectures that handle increased load efficiently without compromising performance are essential., This includes investigating the use of edge computing to distribute computational load and reduce latency, as well as exploring hybrid models that combine cloud and edge resources for optimal performance.

Integrating machine learning techniques into video streaming algorithms can revolutionize the field. Future work could focus on enhancing prediction accuracy for optimal mode selection and content distribution. Predictive analytics can anticipate user behavior, such as viewing patterns and preferences, and adjust streaming strategies accordingly. Reinforcement learning algorithms could be employed to continually adapt streaming policies based on real-time feedback, ensuring the best probable quality of involvement for users. Additionally, deep learning models can be skilled on vast datasets for the purpose of predicting optimal bitrate levels, pre-fetching strategies, and cache management policies, significantly improving the efficiency and reliability of video content delivery systems.

Ensuring consistent Quality of Service (QoS) across different network environments is another significant challenge that future research must address. Adaptive bitrate streaming (ABR) algorithms that enthusiastically adjust video quality on the basis of available bandwidth are crucial., Future studies could explore developing more robust ABR algorithms that consider not only current bandwidth but also predicted network conditions and user device capabilities. This involves creating sophisticated models that predict short-term bandwidth fluctuations and adjust streaming quality proactively. Additionally, research could focus on multi-path streaming techniques that utilize multiple network interfaces to ensure stable and high-grade video delivery level in unstable network conditions.

As peer-to-peer and cloud-based video content downloading systems become more prevalent, ensuring privacy and security is increasingly important. Future work could investigate implementing advanced encryption techniques and robust authentication mechanisms to protect user data and ensure content integrity. Developing new cryptographic protocols optimized for real-time streaming and low-latency environments is essential., Additionally, research could explore using blockchain technology for secure and transparent management of content distribution rights and user access controls. Enhancing privacy and security measures can build more resilient systems which safeguard user data and content from unofficial access and tampering. Exploring these areas in future research endeavors will significantly contribute to the ongoing evolution of video content downloading systems, ultimately leading to enhanced user experiences and improved system performance across diverse network landscapes.

www.ingramcontent.com/pod-product-compliance
Lightning Source LLC
LaVergne TN
LVHW030727061126
851857LV00019B/2022
9781962116794